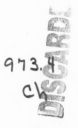

MR. HAMILTON AND MR. JEFFERSON

Mr. Hamilton
and
Mr. Jefferson

Donald Barr Chidsey

THOMAS NELSON INC., PUBLISHERS
Nashville   New York

First edition

Library of Congress Cataloging in Publication Data

Chidsey, Donald Barr.
  Mr. Hamilton and Mr. Jefferson.

  Bibliography: p.
  SUMMARY: Discusses the ideological conflict between Thomas Jefferson and Alexander Hamilton and its effect on the development of the
newly created United States.
  1. United States Politics and government—1789—1792. 2. United States
—Politics and government—1797–1801. 3. Hamilton, Alexander, 1757–
1804. 4. Jefferson, Thomas, Pres. U.S. 1743–1826. [1. Hamilton, Alex-
ander, 1757–1804. 2. Jefferson, Thomas, Pres. U.S., 1743–1797. 3.
United States—Politics and government—1789–1797. 4. United States—
Politics and government—1797–1801] I. Title.
E311.C47   973.4′092′2 [B]   74–34448
ISBN 0–8407–6446–4

★ Contents ★

MR. HAMILTON AND MR. JEFFERSON

★ 1 ★

Everything Was New

★ Five men met in the upstairs drawing room of the Deshler house at 150 High Street, Philadelphia—it was next door to a hairdresser's—the morning of April 19, 1793. They met in order to discuss the most important matter in America.

These men had one thing in common. Without the puffery of self-importance, each knew that whatever he did at this stage of the game might affect the well-being of millions of his fellow countrymen, existent and to come. The nation was new. There were no precedents. The United States, a baby, had been born a republic in a world that consisted almost entirely of lands led by crowned personages who sat on thrones. Could such a government endure? It depended upon these men, and they knew it.

Previous republics, like Venice, like Switzerland or Holland, had been small, compact, homogeneous. The only large one, Rome, when it first started to *get* large, had crashed with a bang that shook the world, to be succeeded by the worst conceivable form of tyranny. What would happen to the American toddler?

Another thing that these five men agreed upon was their hatred and dread of political parties. Only one of them had ever been abroad, but they were well-read men, and they knew about the partisan clashes in split-up Italy and among the cocky, pretentious little duchies and electorates of Germany. They knew too about the confused revolutionary conditions in France, where more parties than you could shake a scythe at were striving to slash one another's throats when they were not busy trying to drag the rest of the continent down to their own bloody level. The five men knew as well that the Great Britain from which they had so recently and so messily been separated was at an all-time political low, the very sink of corruption, nepotism, and vice, largely because of the eye-gouging Whig–Tory bouts that never seemed to cease there. Nothing like that must be permitted to happen in America, where already "party" was a dirty word. The men in the Deshler house were firm on this point.

In fact, in 1793, there were no political parties in the world, at least not political parties as the world knows them today, as history has recorded them. There were cliques and claques and family "connections" that contributed noisily to the woes of mankind, but no organized, dedicated groups of political workers who strove for announced purposes to sway, more or less in unison, their fellowmen. No matter. The very thought of any form of political discipline was repellent to the Founding Fathers. That way, they believed, lay chaos.

The host on this occasion, the President of the United States— a tall broad-shouldered man, preternaturally handsome, shy, solemn—was especially concerned about the possibility that parties might emerge in the new nation. At sixty-one he was the oldest of the five, though erect and muscular, always the soldier. It had been said of his friend, the excitable young Marquis de Lafayette, that he was a statue wandering around looking for a pedestal to stand on. This would never have been said of George Washington, who might have been *born* with that pedestal in place below him, as Pooh-Bah was said to have been born sneering and Richard III with teeth.

Serene the President was still, that morning at 150 High Street, an awesome sight, but inwardly he was unsure of himself. A man of rugged strength and superb courage, seemingly indestructible, he had never until this time doubted that his body would do whatever he called upon it to do. But now he worried, though dutifully he suppressed all signs of it. Were not his eyes failing him, though ever so slightly? Did he hear as well as he used to? For many years he had been troubled by the tendency of his wooden teeth to tumble out at crucial moments, but he had learned to control this condition. What troubled him now was a gnawing fear that he might not prove physically up to the position of Father of His Country. He felt his responsibility. He was, indeed, a slave to it.

He was uncertain, too, about his position, and here he was not alone. The brand-new Senate after a long debate had decided that the President should be addressed as "His Highness the President of the United States and Protector of their Liberties," a title the brand-new House of Representatives refused to accept. Some special deference was due to an office so exalted, though the deference would need to be, like the office itself, new. *Everything* was so new these days. . . . Moreover, this discussion was not confined to the halls of Congress. It had reached the man in the street, who participated in it—so at least the President had come to believe, though it must be admitted that his acquaintanceship with the man in the street was of the skimpiest.

The President valued his popularity as a general, as the steadfast if not brilliant leader of his nation's forces through the years of the Revolution, and it pained him to hear that this popularity might fade now that there was peace in the land. People, it was whispered, had begun to criticize his "monarchical airs."

In the stable behind the Deshler house the President kept, besides his saddle horses, six "muslin horses," white and well matched. When he rode forth on formal occasions, all of these were used to pull the canary-colored chariot he had imported from England—a carriage decorated with gilded nymphs and cupids, and with the Washington arms painted on its doors—though sometimes he used only four horses, and when he went to church with Martha, as he did every Sunday, only two. The hooves of these horses were blackened and their teeth scrubbed before every outing. They were called muslin horses because the head stableman went over every inch of each of them with a piece of white muslin just before they were harnessed, and God help the stable-boy who had the washing detail that day if the cloth afterward showed any smudge. The President saw nothing wrong in this practice. He thought it was no more than his duty to keep it up because of his position. Besides, he loved horses.

The President had heard that men were calling the Deshler house, which he had rented for £700 a year, "the palace." * He resented that. He suspected, too, that sarcastic remarks were made about his "levees," which were held every Tuesday from 3 to 4 P.M. while Congress was in session. These were hardly cheerful occasions. The President, clad in black velvet, his hair freshly powdered, silver buckles at his knees and on his shoes, wore yellow gloves and carried on his left arm a cocked hat with a black feathered fringe. At his side dangled a sword encased in a white leather scabbard. He stood ramrod-stiff while servants ranged the invited visitors, all male, in a loose circle. Then he went around that circle, saying a few words to each man, and after he had finished, they were dismissed. He did not shake anybody's hand. He did not like to shake hands or to touch a man in any other way or be touched by him.

Martha's "drawing rooms," held every Friday evening—but always ending by nine o'clock, because both the Washingtons liked to get to bed early—were more popular. Martha liked to mix with people. The President didn't.

If these matters seem somewhat less than momentous it should be remembered that they were tied in the President's mind with the admittedly graver matter that he was about to take up with

* This house still stands, the address now being 5442 Germantown Avenue. It is owned by the United States government, Department of the Interior, and is located within the National Historical Area of Germantown Avenue. It was built in 1772 by David Deshler, a shipping merchant in the West Indies trade, and is generally called the Deshler House or the Deshler–Morris House. It is open to the public, a showplace. Sir William Howe made it his headquarters soon after the Battle of Germantown. In Washington's time it was probably called the Deshler House or perhaps the Frank House, for it was owned then (1792–93) by Colonel Isaac Frank, the President's landlord. It did not come into the possession of the Morris family until after the turn of the century.

his heads of department, who were threatening to split the government into parties, to cause the emergence of an opposition group. Opposition, as things stood in Philadelphia, the capital, would be sedition, and could lead only to catastrophe.

No doubt George Washington had all this in mind when he called the meeting to order.

★ 2 ★

Two Cocks in a Pit

★ The Constitution authorized the President to "require the opinion, in writing, of the principal officer in each of the executive departments, upon any subject relating to the duties of their respective offices," and this he proposed to do. He was always willing to take advice, or at least to seek it. During the Revolution he had never hesitated to call a council of war when some important military decision was to be made. He believed this to be his duty.

There were four of them, and they did not think of themselves as a Cabinet. The Constitution did not use that word, which to the men who assembled at the Deshler house seemed faintly malodorous, being European. The President thought of them as department heads, and they thought of themselves as Secretaries, though one, the Treasury man, Alexander Hamilton, preferred to be referred to as Chancellor or even, sometimes, as Prime Minister.

Because the group was so small, the President had made sure it was balanced. One man came from Massachusetts, one from New York, and two from Virginia. Division, separation, always threatened, could ruin the land.

Henry Knox, the Secretary of War, had been beefy even as a boy; as a man, now forty-three, he was enormous, weighing close to three hundred pounds. He waddled when he walked, and un-

14

derlings and associates made fun of his pomposity. Like that other doughty general of the Revolution, Nathanael Greene, he had been an ardent young Sunday-drilling militiaman who read everything about the military art that he could get his hands on. In Knox's case these books were many, and conveniently located, for he had been the proprietor of the London Book-Store in Boston before he joined the Continental Army as chief of artillery. He was not brilliant, but the soldiers had liked him and he was a good organizer, a man who got things done. His bellow was famous, a quarterdeck voice, and men still told of how on that momentous night of December 25, 1776, he had outhowled the gale that tore down the valley of the Delaware as he supervised the loading of his cannons in Durham boats for the trip to Trenton. He had seen all sorts of action—Bunker Hill, the siege of Boston, Morristown, Valley Forge, Monmouth, Yorktown. Already a full colonel when the war started, he had finished as a major general. He became Washington's successor as Commander-in-Chief after peace came, and then, later, the first Secretary of War. He seldom had much to say at the meetings of the heads of departments, and the others paid scant attention to what he did. In war he had been Washington's man, firmly, unwaveringly, through everything, but in politics he was Hamilton's. He fairly worshiped the Secretary of the Treasury.

Hamilton was a crisp little man. He was a prodigy who had come up from the West Indies, where he had been a storekeeper as a mere boy. "Meteoric" is the word customarily applied to his rise, though nobody ever denied that he deserved it.

Everybody who knew him, even those from his earliest days in the sugar islands, had assumed that Hamilton was marked for greatness. But—how? In what field? Just to look at him, even in youth, you knew that there was genius in him, genius, moreover, that he would be unlikely to try to hide. Small he was, yes, but trim, dapper, in all things utterly sure of himself. He had a pale face lightly sprinkled with freckles, and damn-you eyes, eyes the color of steel on a cloudy day. His chin jutted up and out as though he would shovel you aside with it. Impatience fairly piped

within him, like steam threatening an explosion. Surely, you said
to yourself, this person is about to do something stupendous. But,
again, *what?*

At first it had been supposed that Hamilton would set the world
on fire as a literary man. In writing as in speech he possessed what
seemed a God-given sense of direction. He could and infallibly
did go right to the core of every matter that he took up, and he
could spread his findings convincingly, with nothing left to be said,
the argument closed. True, he was coercive rather than persuasive.
He used the stick rather than the carrot. But he got results.

It was a piece of writing that first brought him to the attention
of his elders and got him out of the West Indies and into the great
world of the British mainland colonies, where he could shine. At
fifteen the manager of a trading house branch in St. Croix, Virgin
Islands, he wrote a description of a hurricane that had just passed.
It was perfervid stuff, but the local newspaper, *The Royal Danish-
American Gazette,* published it. A Presbyterian padre hailed it as
a masterpiece and started to collect funds to send the *Wunder-
kind* to college.

No man today could read that composition without wincing, but
it was esteemed tasteful in its time, and certainly it was a triumph
for a lad of fifteen. That the precocious one was a love child—the
offspring of a French woman who had recently died and a Scottish
aristocrat, a bankrupt who had disappeared—made the pastor's
task the easier. But it was Hamilton's amazing record as a trader
that most interested the moneymen and in particular young Cor-
nelius Kortright, a partner of the powerful New York trader
Nicholas Cruger. Kortright, who virtually underwrote Hamilton's
venture, was himself a young man. His inheritance, Kortright &
Co., owned, among many other things, all of the farming land that
later became Columbia University.

After passing through Boston and New York, Hamilton went
first to the New Jersey College at Princeton, a Presbyterian establishment, because he had a letter to its president, Dr. Witherspoon, from his clerical sponsor in Christiansted, Dr. Hugh Knox.
When old Dr. Witherspoon refused to change the rules in such a

way as to let him zip through Princeton in record time, Hamilton, a young man in a hurry, went instead to King's College (now Columbia) in New York City, where he *did* zip through. In Hamilton's time the institution was located downtown, being bounded by Church, Barclay, Greenwich, and Murray streets, and had a faculty of three. It was Church of England.

Even while Hamilton was a student and still in his teens, he was an enthusiastic member of the Hearts of Oak, a group of young men who wore green with brown leather facings and drilled on the common whenever classes permitted. Was he fated then to be a great military man, a conqueror? For a little time it seemed so. When the war came, he joined up as soon as the guns started to boom. He became a captain of artillery and saw action at Trenton. He burned with military ardor. He imagined he heard the flapping of battle standards above him, the shrieks of the wounded below, and like some imaginative schoolboy he pictured himself leading his men up a slope to charge a seemingly impregnable position. He saw himself waving his sword, shouting encouragement to the others, the shadowy ones behind him, for he was determined to do or to die. He had just turned twenty.

Hamilton's virtues, his stouthearted courage, his verve and élan, remained hidden, but when somebody at headquarters learned that the youngster had a head for figures, wrote a good hand, was fluent with words, and even knew a little French, he was appointed an aide to General Washington, to be a secretary, a letter writer, with the rank of lieutenant colonel, no less. He hated it, but he did a good job.

It has been estimated that just after the Revolution slightly fewer than two out of every one thousand adult white male Americans had ever been to a college, but it seemed to George Washington that almost all of those around him were in that class. He was acutely conscious of his own education, a somewhat hit-or-miss affair instilled into him by a succession of tutors. Not for him were the groves of Academe, and he regretted it. Most of all, he believed that he could not write well. He was mistaken in that, because he wrote readily, in a plain, forceful style. If his letters lacked fashionable polish, a quality that he thought he owed to his position, their meaning was always clear.

The writing of letters was a very important part of any important man's life in those days, and Washington, though he turned out thousands, found it an onerous chore. He welcomed young Hamilton, who would listen for a few minutes to what he had to say and then turn it into a series of letters that exactly expressed what was in the general's mind.

Hamilton was always there; he seemed never to sleep. He was neat, exact, and fast. But all the while he was dreaming of the blood-wet battlefield, the bullets whistling, the flourished sword. Repeatedly he asked to be transferred to an active nonclerical command, and repeatedly Washington, who was very good to him, talked him out of it. At last the two quarreled, but Alexander Hamilton sooner or later quarreled with almost everyone he knew. In their case, the aide, prickly as a porcupine, believed that he had been summoned in too peremptory a manner, treated almost like a servant, and he complained loudly and in writing. There was no threat of a challenge—that would have been preposterous—but despite the general's efforts at conciliation, which approached a downright apology, relations remained strained, and at last Lieutenant Colonel Hamilton's resignation was accepted. Hamilton returned to New York State, married money, and began to have children. He took a crash course in law and, by special dispensation, was admitted to the bar, emulating in his actions another bright young New Yorker, Aaron Burr.

Hamilton's pull was his father-in-law, Philip Schuyler, a large landowner and one of the first members of the United States Senate. Burr's pull was his family name. He was a grandson of Jonathan Edwards, the son of a former president of Princeton, his own alma mater. Both Hamilton and Burr made the course in less than half a year, thanks to special legislation.

During this time Hamilton had not forgotten the war. He was elected by the New York legislature to the Continental Congress, where he served briefly, but all the while he was pushing his application for a colonel's commission in the army. The commission came through in time to allow him to lead a regiment south to the Yorktown peninsula, where Cornwallis was stoppered with a military cork. By special permission of the Commander-in-Chief, who had long since forgiven him his youthful bad manners, he was appointed over several others with longer records to attack and take one of the two redoubts that must be made to fall before a British surrender could be expected. He did this and did it very well. He waved that sword at last, and won a smashing victory. Little though he was, he arranged to have a trooper hump over at the outside of the redoubt wall, and he vaulted to this man's back and from thence into the fortification itself, the first to get there. Then the war was over, for all practical purposes, and he went back to New York and the practice of law.

New York, a growing port, had been in the hands of the British throughout the Revolution and for some time afterward, so that there were many residents, especially those in the professional class, upon whom the taint of Toryism had been cast, making them exiles. All sorts of property disputes remained to be settled, and New York was wide open to any young lawyer who, like Hamilton, had sound patriotic affiliations.

Yet even his admirers could not picture Alexander Hamilton as a great lawyer or lawgiver. He had a propensity to lecture, to talk down to his hearers as he waggled an admonitory forefinger, and jurors did not enjoy this. His briefs were marvels of lucidity and force, but when he spoke in argument his voice, always reedy, too often became a screech. Also, he could be unbearably long-winded, a curious fault for him, and one that never showed in his writings. In short, though he was successful from the beginning, it seemed unlikely that he would supplant Blackstone as a legal colossus.

Money: That was the answer. Figures. Trade. Until Robert Morris proposed him to Washington as the first Secretary of the Treasury nobody, including the man himself, seems to have suspected that Alexander Hamilton was a financial wizard. But he was. He picked up the Treasury Department, as left by the Articles of Confederation government, and found it a sorry mess. He shook it, brushed it off, injected into it some mysterious stimulant of which he alone had the recipe, and sent it on its whooping way, a dazzling delight.

He did not stop there. Obsessed, as always, with the belief that only Alexander Hamilton could run things as they should be run, he took over the War Department as well, his fat friend General Knox bobbing in agreement. Hamilton also never hesitated to give a legal opinion, whether asked or not, on anything that he thought might be troubling the President, and often this opinion prevailed over that of the Attorney General, Edmund Randolph.

As for the State Department, Hamilton simply ignored it, bypassed it, offering his advice on international matters directly to the President. He held almost daily conferences with the British ambassador,* and in his official capacity corresponded with highly placed acquaintances in England and in Canada. Indeed, the "Prime Minister" had things much his own way at Cabinet meetings—until March 21, 1790, when Thomas Jefferson returned from France and reported to President Washington as the first Secretary of State. Then things began to change.

These two men, whose enmity was to alter and shape the course of our country, could not have been more ludicrously unlike one another if they had been selected, appareled, and rehearsed by some celestial stage manager who strove for dramatic effect.

Moreau de St. Mery, who met Hamilton in 1794 just after

---

* Ambassador Extraordinary and Plenipotentiary is the highest rank in diplomatic service, followed by Envoy Extraordinary, Minister Plenipotentiary, and Chargé d'Affaires.

It was the practice in early days for large countries to exchange ambassadors with one another and ministers with smaller and less important countries. For the first century of her existence, the United States was one of these smaller and less important countries, and consequently her official diplomatic representatives abroad were Ministers Plenipotentiary.

However, "minister" is too easily confused with the cabinet officers of other governments ("foreign minister") and with clerics ("minister of the gospel"). So for the purposes of this book, the term "ambassador" has been applied to *all* officially accredited diplomats.

Hamilton had resigned as Secretary of the Treasury, described him thus in his *American Journey:*

He was small, with an extremely composed bearing, unusually small eyes, and something a little furtive in his glance. He spoke French, but quite incorrectly. He had a great deal of ready wit, kept a close watch over himself, and was, I repeat, extremely brave. He had no desire for private gain, but was eaten up with ambition, and ardently admired the laws and government of England, and its financial system. Personally he was very much of an autocrat, and an ardent guardian of the prerogatives of the Executive.

Jefferson was Hamilton's senior, by fourteen years. He stood 6 feet 2½ inches in his stockings and loomed like an untidy giant over pert little Hamilton. He was a pacifist, whereas Hamilton was all fight, even when there was nothing to fight about. Jefferson was slow-spoken, soft-spoken, a man who never raised his voice, though his words could sting. Those who met him for the first time complained that he was cold, aloof, though he proved to be the kindest of men, thoughtful, helpful, a warm friend, the sponger's delight, a soft touch for anybody.

His aspect was that of a teen-ager, all legs; his clothes seemed too small for him. When he sat—though the man was lean—he seemed to overflow the chair. He would cock his head quizzically, his blue eyes ashuttle, one shoulder hunched high, while he listened—and he was a good listener. He was a plain-faced man, who might be called homely. He certainly lacked the silken graces of the courtier, though his manners were impeccable. His mouth was firm, his face ruddy, his nose large. Like Hamilton he was a redhead, but his hair was a slightly darker, a more definite red than that of the Secretary of the Treasury, which was rather sandy, and he never powdered it.

Whether by economic standards or those of heredity, Jefferson rated as a gentleman. His father had been no more than a successful farmer, but his mother had been a Randolph of Virginia. He owned more than 10,000 acres of farmland and about fifty slaves, and he was deeply in debt. Yet he was instinctively a democrat. He was a man who believed in equality of opportunity for all. He trusted his fellow Americans.

After Washington—and not far after—Thomas Jefferson was the oldest man in that second-floor drawing room the morning of April 19, 1793. After Washington, too, he was the most distinguished. He was the best educated of them all, the only one who had been to Europe. Violinist, architect, author, philosopher, botanist, geologist, anthropologist, lawyer, and dirt farmer, he was the most versatile. His shambling, unimpressive presence misled nobody, for he was known to be stubborn, a man who meant to get his own way.

This was more than a mere clash of personalities, this Jefferson—Hamilton relation. It was a fundamental difference of opinion as to what the Constitution of the United States *was*.

Neither man had helped notably to frame the instrument. Jefferson had been in France at the time of the convention of 1787, though he had kept in close touch with the proceedings through his correspondence with his protégé, James Madison. Madison, the "Father of the Constitution," saw the whole thing through, recording every step and each part of every step, and Jefferson thought well of the result. Even if there were a few things he might have changed, he regarded it as an interesting experiment, a compact among the thirteen states from which any of them, after giving proper notice, could withdraw.

Jefferson believed that the Constitution gave the federal government police powers to be used only in an emergency and of course the authority to deal with other nations. He believed that this central government had no other powers excepting those specifically assigned to it by the states, and that even those powers were *lent*, a temporary arrangement, not *given*. Yet although the Constitution might or might not prove to be permanent—only time would tell—Jefferson believed that while it was in force, while it existed, it should be accepted literally, not strained or warped in any way. He was, that is, a strict constructionist.

Hamilton had been a delegate to the 1787 convention in Philadelphia, but through no guilt of his own he had contributed nothing to its product. Governor Clinton of New York had felt obliged to appoint him as a delegate, but he disliked Hamilton personally and distrusted his ideas about a strong central government. Therefore he had appointed as Hamilton's fellow delegates two firm believers in states' rights. One or the other of these men was always on hand to vote the opposite of the way young Hamilton voted, thus under the rules of the convention negating the New York vote, so that all of Hamilton's work went to waste.

Disgusted, Hamilton had absented himself from many of the later sessions in order to take care of his neglected law business in New York, though he did make one epochal speech in which he set forth his own personal opinion. This speech lasted five hours. In a voice that even at the beginning was squeaky, nerve-rasping, he announced that he did not care for either of the two plans being considered by the convention, Virginia's large-state plan, or New Jersey's small-state plan, so he had prepared one of his own, which he would read to them. Before he got around to this reading, however, he talked for several hours, explaining that he did not think they would like it and that he did not mean formally to present it to the convention. At last he read the thing, a paean of praise for the British government, which, the speaker informed the startled delegates, was the best in the world.

It was late, but he still had the floor. His own plan, he explained, called for an Assembly and a Senate, the Assemblymen to be elected directly by the people for three years, the Senators to be elected by electors elected by the people and to serve for life. The executive authority would be vested in a governor, to be elected by electors, who would serve for life. The governor would have extraordinary powers. He would be commander-in-chief of all armed forces. He could make treaties, single-handed, with foreign governments. He would appoint, and could remove at will, all state governors. He would have an absolute veto, from which no appeal was possible, over all legislation, national *and* state.

Hamilton explained all this and much, much more. When he

was finished, nobody said anything. Hamilton then pocketed his bulky plan rather sheepishly, instead of putting it on the president's desk. After a while somebody moved that they adjourn, and they did.

Nevertheless, Hamilton fought for ratification of the Constitution, once the convention had adopted a plan of its own. New York was a pivotal state, and despite the governor's enmity for him, and despite his own pronounced distaste for politics, Alexander Hamilton was a power in New York. Together with James Madison, Thomas Jefferson's most ardent disciple, and with an occasional assist by the ultraconservative John Jay—"Those who own the country ought to govern it"—he turned out *The Federalist* papers, arguing variously and brilliantly in favor of ratification. In addition, when the matter came before a state convention at Poughkeepsie, though in the beginning the Clinton forces numbered 46 to the Hamilton–Madison 19, so skillfully did Hamilton stall the proceedings again and again, so tirelessly did he talk while lieutenants cajoled delegates "out of doors," that eventually, somehow, by one vote, the thing was done; the union was saved.

Hamilton did not think much of what he was given to work with—the Constitution in his eyes was a feeble thing and altogether too democratic—but he believed that he had found a legal loophole through which he and his grandiose plans for a strong central government could slip. The Constitution just adopted, he pointed out, had conferred upon Congress the right "to make all laws which shall be necessary and proper for carrying into execution the foregoing powers, and all other powers vested by the Constitution in the Government of the United States, or in any department or officer thereof." The Secretary of State, the Secretary of the Treasury reminded their associates, interpreted this word "necessary" conventionally as meaning "absolutely" or "indispensably" needed, whereas in fact "*necessary* often means no more than *needful, requisite, incidental, useful,* or *conducive to.*" Since all proper means could not be comprehended beforehand, "the powers contained in a constitution of government, especially those which concern the general administration of the affairs of a country, its finances, trade, defence, etc., ought to be construed liberally in advancement of the public good." In other words, the central government could do just about anything it pleased.

This was known as the doctrine of implied powers, and Hamilton seems to have convinced the President of its validity; but it scared Thomas Jefferson.

So these two men faced one another in meeting after meeting of the Cabinet, "like pitted cocks," as Jefferson himself put it.

The fifth man present that morning was the Attorney General, Edmund Randolph. He was a Virginia gentleman and Washington's close friend. But, indeed he was everybody's friend. He was a man who couldn't seem to say no; he was unconquerably agreeable. To your face he would endorse anything, and warmly, but a moment later you might overhear him endorsing the very opposite thing to somebody else. He was a weathercock, swinging this way and that. He was a straddler. So careful was he to keep his votes evenly spread that the Secretary of State used to complain to friends that Cabinet meetings invariably resulted in a vote of 1½ to 2½, with Knox always with Hamilton and Randolph splitting his vote. The President customarily decided for the majority.

★ 3 ★

Politics as Usual

★ It had begun with a deal. What was to become a yawning chasm between Hamilton and Jefferson, a gulch as deep and as fraught with peril as the Grand Canyon of Arizona, was at the start a sunny plain.

A few years earlier, on a bright March morning in 1790, Thomas Jefferson had just returned from France and was about to accept the post of Secretary of State in the new constitutional government. He did so reluctantly, for he was tired of public life and longed to get back to the farm. Nevertheless, although he did not have an appointment, he went to call upon President Washington.

In front of the house that the Father of his Country had rented in Cherry Street, a pleasant if small thoroughfare in New York City, then the capital, Jefferson encountered the Secretary of the Treasury. Alexander Hamilton, likewise without an appointment, was also about to call upon the President. Hamilton looked unsure of himself, which was not characteristic, and when the two started to chat, it became apparent to the older man that his companion was deeply troubled about something.

They had of course met before, these two, but this was their

26

first talk. Hamilton, self-sufficient though he ordinarily was, must have felt at least a twinge of awe toward this tall statesman so recently returned from Europe, where his accomplishments were fabled. As for Jefferson, though customarily inclined to be stiff with a new acquaintance, he was by instinct kindly to younger men. Many times, later, the Secretary of the Treasury was to refer to the Secretary of State as "that cool, casuistic, Frenchified fellow," but this morning before the President's residence he found him very helpful.

Hamilton had had a head start of more than half a year over Jefferson when it came to gathering power in the new government, and he was not a man to waste time. Responsibilities were not yet clearly defined or jurisdictions clearly allocated, and Hamilton had been eager to accept more than his share. His office was the busiest, as it was the largest, of any department. Besides those who worked directly under him, he had the customs administration well in hand, with literally hundreds of clerks, inspectors, and such —the biggest single chunk of patronage. In addition, he had friends in each of the two houses of Congress as well as influential followers—Uriah Tracy of Connecticut, Jonathan Dayton of New Jersey, Theodore Sedgwick of Massachusetts, and his own father-in-law, General Philip Schuyler, who was in the Senate—who were glad to push any measures he proposed. All the same, he told the Secretary of State, he was worried.

Nobody had known, really, how much money the states and the national government owed when Hamilton took over Treasury, except that it was a great deal. He soon came up with a figure: $54,124,464.56. Nearly all of this sum had grown out of the Revolutionary War.

The foreign debt—owed to the governments of France and Spain, France's being by far the bigger, and also to certain private bankers in the Netherlands—amounted to $11.7 million, which included $1.6 million of defaulted interest. The $42 million domestic debt included overdue interest of $13 million, the great bulk of it consisting of 6 percent certificates issued to settle army

pay and farmers' and contractors' claims for war supplies and
services.

These glittering sums Alexander Hamilton tossed into the air
and caught again as deftly as a prestidigitator tosses glass balls.
They probably meant about as much as that to Thomas Jefferson,
who, however, nodded gravely. Jefferson was a member of many
learned societies, a lawyer, a philosopher, and very well read,
but he had no head for figures.

Hamilton's money schemes were many, and they were connected. They interlocked, being interdependent upon one another,
so that he was to insist, all along, that he must have every one of
them enacted, complete as he had presented it, or else none.

The plan was grand. However, Hamilton told Secretary Jefferson only about the first part of it as they walked Cherry Street
that fine morning, pacing back and forth in front of the President's house, and that was just as well. Secretary Jefferson assuredly would have taken alarm if he'd heard it all. Hamilton
believed that the national government should consolidate the
whole debt, state and national, foreign and domestic, and turn it
over to the tender care of professional financiers. He believed that
Mammon helps those who help themselves. He believed, passionately, that the central government should subsidize not farmers, who would go on raising their crops anyway, but rather manu-
facturers and, even more, traders, the moneymen, who would
thus be encouraged to spend—and make—even more money. He
could be classed as one of the first subscribers to the so-called
trickle-down doctrine: Give to the rich, and the others will eventually get their share, more or less. All of which would have
horrified Thomas Jefferson.

That day on Cherry Street the Secretary of State was informed
only of the first part of the grand plan, the refunding part. Hamilton sought to have the central government take over all of the
debts of the states. He would pay off all claims at the face value of
the certificates, though many of these, perhaps most of them, had
been bought up from war veterans and indigent farmers by

speculators who paid only a few cents on the dollar. Thus, the moneymen could become a part of the government, as it were, its interests their interests. And it should be done, Hamilton thought, in order to establish the national credit. He did not tell Secretary Jefferson (though he knew) where he meant to get the money with which to do this; nor did Jefferson ask him—that could wait.

Hamilton's immediate concern was his refunding bill, presently before Congress, where it faced hard sledding. Mr. Jefferson, though not himself a member of Congress, had much influence among the members, especially those from the southern states. Couldn't these two perhaps come to some arrangement? Only a few votes were needed in order to swing the refunding deal, without which the whole business would crash. The little man paused for an answer.

Jefferson seems not to have hesitated. He invited Secretary Hamilton to have breakfast with him the next morning, so they could talk it over.

Lunch had not yet been invented. Breakfast was the best meal at which businessmen and politicians might discuss their affairs. Dinner, in mid- or late afternoon—the time changed, depending upon fashion—was too filling and too heavily attended, a family occasion. Supper was late, and many men were drunk or dead tired by that time. Breakfast was best. It was the accepted practice.

Hamilton was there on time, and he might have been momentarily abashed when he learned that James Madison was to be another guest, but if he was, he concealed it.

Madison, a close personal friend of the Secretary of State and, like Jefferson, a Virginia country gentleman, was in appearance the most improbable of the Founding Fathers. He was small, short, neat to a turn, homely, precise. He always seemed unsure of himself, though he wasn't. He had done more than any other man to write the new Constitution and to see it adopted. His patriotism was pure, his intellect keen, his energy, it would seem, boundless. Looking at him, one might have found it hard to take the man seriously; yet he was a heroic fighter for the rights of his fellow countrymen. If Thomas Jefferson is called (as he has been) the father of the Democratic Party of the United States, then James Madison could be called the grandfather.

Madison might be considered the leader of the opposition at this time, if there had been anybody willing to admit the existence of an opposition. He was the most alert and the most hardworking man in the House of Representatives. Though a coauthor of *The Federalist* papers, with Hamilton, he was opposed to Hamilton's plans for a strong central government, and he thought that the refunding program would be a bad mistake. He had pointed out more than once that it would be the poor man who would suffer, the rich man who would profit. He did not believe in the trickledown theory.

Ever ready with a compromise solution, however, Madison had suggested from the floor of the House a sort of sliding-scale refunding plan of his own, by which only the original holders of the securities would be refunded at the face value of what they held. The others, the speculators, would get back only what they had paid.

Hamilton had brushed this idea aside. Unthinkable, he had said.

Hamilton certainly knew—as did Madison, though Jefferson perhaps did not yet—that more than four fifths of the national debt was owed to men who lived north of the Potomac. Except for South Carolina, most of the state debts were in the North. Maryland, Georgia, North Carolina owed little; Pennsylvania owed about $2 million; New York, New Jersey, Massachusetts, and South Carolina had large debts; Delaware had none; Virginia owed about $3 million. It seemed natural, then, that New England and the middle states would approve such a refunding plan, while the southern states would oppose it. That, of course, was why Hamilton was angling for southern votes. He needed, in particular, House votes.

The host came directly to the point. Secretary Hamilton had said what he *wanted,* but what was he prepared to *give?* After all, it was he who had asked for this conference.

Hamilton replied that he would give the national capital.

The need to settle upon some city or some site for a permanent capital was generally recognized. Congress had recently decided that the capital should be moved from New York City to Philadelphia for ten years. New York, which had just spent $50,000 to overhaul and redecorate the old City Hall on Wall Street at the head of Broad Street, which thereupon became Federal Hall (it is the present Sub-Treasury Building), had opposed this move.

Just the same, the thing would soon be done. Many Philadelphians had even been working quietly to get an agreement in Congress to keep the capital in the City of Brotherly Love after the ten years had elapsed, but it looked at the moment as though this movement was doomed. Nearby places—Germantown, Chester—had been proposed. Two towns occupied by the Second Continental Congress in emergencies, when the British had threatened or taken Philadelphia—namely, Lancaster, Pennsylvania, and Baltimore, Maryland—were mentioned. There was a great deal of behind-the-scenes dickering about it, a great deal of politicking. Also, some Southerners thought that the capital should be farther south, in Virginia, for instance, or somewhere on the Potomac, Georgetown being favorably mentioned.

Jefferson understood Hamilton's suggestion. Yes, that would be a fair swap. He could promise the House votes of Richard Bland Lee and Alexander White, Virginians who owned property on the Potomac. They would vote for refunding if he asked them to. He *thought* that he could get Daniel Carroll and George Gale of Maryland as well, but he was *sure* of White and Lee.

Hamilton agreed. He also agreed to swing the New York delegation, a crucial one, in favor of the Potomac plan.

Madison did not approve, but because he worshiped Thomas Jefferson, he did promise that although he would not vote *for* refunding himself, at least he would cease to work *against* it.

So it was settled. The deal was made. Hamilton got his refunding plan, and the American people eventually got Washington, D.C.

Afterward, after he had learned what Alexander Hamilton was getting at, what he meant to make the American government into, Jefferson was to cry angrily that he had been "tricked" into this deal. But that was not true. He had known perfectly well what he was doing. He was just a poor loser.

★ 4 ★

A Lawyer Finds a Loophole

★ Only a few days before the meeting, on April 19, 1793, between Washington and his Cabinet, the President had learned that war had broken out in Europe. France had gone mad. It was not a mannered madness, a gentle shove over the lip of despair, but a real raging mania, a frothing-at-the-mouth fury. France had gone *stark staring* mad.

Imitation, it has been said, is the sincerest form of flattery, and just at first Americans on the whole had been pleased to see the French people go on a republican spree. They had warmed to the cries of *Liberté, Égalité, Fraternité* that came across the water, for, fresh from their own revolution, they liked to think that they had inspired a world movement in that path, and that France's carrying on of a torch signaled the end of monarchy, titles, and special privileges for the highborn and rich.

Not a few people had become silly on the subject, and went about wearing tricolor cockades, greeting one another in the street as "Citizen" and "Citizeness," or sometimes even "Citess." These enthusiasts ran the French flag up on their poles alongside the Stars and Stripes. In Boston and Charleston, in Philadelphia and New York—for this was largely a city fever—they sang "The Marseillaise" and "Ça Ira," danced the carmagnole, and celebrated July 14 (Bastille Day) with fully the fervor that they ex-

33

hibited on their own July 4 (Independence Day). They had passed resolutions in favor of the revolution, and whenever France won a victory in the field of Mars—something that France was doing rather frequently in those days—they hailed it in tricolor-swagged banqueting halls with toast after valiant toast.

Some few less demonstrative souls sought to justify their adherence to the cause of the *sans culottes* by asserting that they were thinking of the future and of the well-being of their own country. The United States had no navy—the last vessel of the old Continental Navy had been sold in 1784—but France and Great Britain had enormous navies. The destiny of the new young nation lay in the North Atlantic. Therefore, when Great Britain and France were at war, as they virtually always were, the United States, in order to live, must take one side or the other.

Almost everybody was agreed upon that. But the Francophiles pointed out that France had helped us in our moment of direst need. They said we were bound to that country not only by treaty but by moral obligations. In any event, these fellows said, the French Revolution was the wave of the future. Soon it would envelop all of Europe, then all the world, sounding aristocracy's death knell. Better get aboard while the getting was good.

The Franco*phobes* answered this argument by asserting that the French Revolution was already doomed. The kings of Europe were combining their forces in order to stamp it out. Better get away from that revolution—far away. Better pretend that never for an instant had you taken it seriously.

The Gallomen and the Anglomen—opposites—were both sincerely patriotic.

For a little while two developments seemed to dampen the ardor of the American believers in antimonarchism. The French, being French, overdid the business, and their behavior gave some Gallomen pause. In December of 1792, the revolutionists over there had announced the creation of a French republic, and to most Americans this seemed fair enough, a natural development. However, on January 21 (though the news did not reach the United States until late in March) they cut off the head of their prisoner-king, Louis XVI, and even to many Gallomen that seemed like carrying matters too far. The revolutionists had also lopped off the head of Louis's blond Austrian wife, Marie Antoinette, but this event did not jolt Americans as harshly as had the execution of the king himself. After all, while the man might not have been bright—and it was whispered that he drank too much—Louis XVI had been a generous friend to America when America desperately needed a friend. He had already been stripped of his power, and even of his titles, so why kill him? Did it mean that the revolution over there was indeed, as the Anglomen contended, degenerating into savagery? Was this what the democratic march-on was coming to?

The second reason for perturbation was that France's belligerency was no longer confined to France. The new revolutionists, it appeared, wanted to fight everybody in sight. They were not satisfied to keep *Liberté, Égalité, Fraternité* to themselves, but sought to jam it down the throat of every people in Europe. The French had fought Prussia and beaten her soundly at Valmy, September 20 of the previous year, but Prussia was not a mercantile nation, not a power with a navy, and the news of the battle meant little in America, though it did give the Gallomen an excuse for some additional victory dinners.

But now France was going further. Only the other day, April 7, Thomas Jefferson in his role of Secretary of State had notified President Washington that France had declared war on Great Britain and also on Holland. Spain was sure to follow, such was the European setup, and who knew how many others? Was there any possible way, now, for the the United States to stay away from the maelstrom?

More immediately alarming was the news that an ambassador was on his way from France, one Edmond Charles Édouard Genêt, a young man Jefferson had known slightly while in that country. Genêt might appear in Philadelphia, complete with credentials, any day now. Should he be received officially? Would that be an act of unfriendliness to Great Britain, with whom the new French republic was at war? Would it not indicate acceptance of the killing of King Louis as a *fait accompli,* implying approval? In either case, wouldn't it involve the United States in a war the nation so obviously could not afford?

It was to answer these questions and others like them that Washington had called this meeting of the Cabinet.

Like all of the other meetings it quickly resolved itself into a debate between the Secretary of State and the Secretary of the Treasury, with the Secretary of the Treasury doing most of the talking.

To Hamilton the whole thing was crystal clear. Four fifths of our foreign trade, both import and export, was with Great Britain or some British colony. England had the larger navy and could easily cut off our total trade with France, such as that was. France was three thousand miles away, but in Canada Great Britain had a long land boundary with us, and despite the terms of the peace treaty that had ended the Revolution, she still maintained garrisons in the various western forts that guarded the St. Lawrence and the Lakes, so that she could at any time attack us by means of the back door whilst the Royal Navy attacked us from the front, thus obliterating us. A war with Great Britain would be fatal.

A war with France would not hurt much immediately and in the long run might well benefit the United States as having been a member of the winning coalition. Hamilton was sure, as were all of the other Anglomen, that the kings and princes and grand dukes of Europe, momentarily discomfited, were drawing together and would soon strike tellingly against the French madness. The President certainly should issue a proclamation of neutrality, as he was proposing to do, and should flatly refuse to receive this man Genêt.

Thomas Jefferson demurred. The trade with France and particularly that with the French West Indian colonies was by no means inconsiderable, and it was growing. He said: "Besides five-eighths of our whale oil and two-thirds of our salted fish, they take from us one-fourth of our tobacco, three-fourths of our live stock . . . a considerable and growing portion of our rice. . . ." But enough of mercantilism! France was our friend, and an envoy from France should be treated *as* a friend. The issuance of a proclamation of neutrality, Jefferson thought, would be a hostile act, unworthy of the republic of the United States. Besides, went on this strict constructionist, the Constitution, gave the right to make war to the Congress, not to the Executive Deparment, and certainly a declaration of no war—that is, of neutrality—came under this head.

All this sounded suspiciously like an application of the doctrine of implied powers, but the father of the doctrine, its distinguished sponsor, its expositor, denied it vehemently. War making might be the prerogative of the legislature, the Secretary of the Treasury announced, but the keeping of the *peace* was that of the President.

Here the President himself cautiously interposed a suggestion that Ambassador Genêt might be received though "not with too much warmth or cordiality," but nobody paid attention to this.

Washington was distressed to see the meeting turn into yet another spat between its two cleverest members, but there was nothing that he could do. Hamilton had been well prepared for this encounter, and indeed, he had probably proposed it in the first place. He had framed most of the questions the President was asking, and he had an answer for everything.

Jefferson nevertheless persisted. When he got a chance, he broke in with a reminder that the United States, after all, was bound to France by treaties of amity and commerce, both signed February 6, 1778. Men might assert—men had—that the all-but-crushed colonies at that time would have signed such a pact with the Devil himself if the Devil had been in a position to rescue them, and that France had not been obeying any warmhearted impulse to help the American colonies attain independence but rather had been intent upon embarrassing her old enemy England. However, the fact remained that we *had* signed such treaties and that France had lived up to her part of them and now for the first time was asking our aid. To turn away Monsieur Genêt, Jefferson warned, would be to break our word of honor.

No such thing, cried Hamilton. He was braced against this argument. The lawyer already had his loophole. The treaties of

amity and commerce, he pointed out, had been signed with the
crown of France. There no longer was a crown of France. Do
treaties bind nations, peoples, and not just governments? Of
course not. Therefore, these treaties should be "temporarily and
provisionally suspended," if not abrogated.

Hamilton went further. Clearly what France was seeking, he
said, was an admission on the part of the United States of their
obligations under Article 22 of the Treaty of Amity, which article
would give harborage and restocking rights in American ports to
French privateers or warships whilst denying them to the vessels
of nations with which France might happen to be at war. But—
the French treaties had been specified as *defensive* treaties, and
now France was fighting an *offensive* war, a war that *she* had
declared; therefore the obligation no longer existed.

The spate of words went on and on. After hours of wrangling
it was agreed that Genêt should indeed be received, but without
warmth. Washington would see to that.

It was also agreed, despite Jefferson's objection, that the President should issue a proclamation of neutrality. It would not be
called that—indeed, in deference to Jefferson, the word "neutrality" would not occur anywhere in this message, which the
Attorney General would draw up—but that was what it would
amount to.

The other questions, which were of lesser importance, were
left unanswered.

This was a Friday. On Monday the proclamation was issued
over Washington's signature. It enjoined Americans to refrain from
any act or attitude that might benefit any one European belligerent at the expense of any other, and specifically forbade them to
accept commissions in any European military force or to serve in
any other capacity in such a force. It started: "Whereas it appears that a state of war exists between Austria, Prussia, Sardinia,
Great Britain, and the United Netherlands, of the one part, and
France on the other . . ." It did not mention Spain, Portugal, or
Russia, though President Washington and his advisers surely be-

lieved that these nations would get into the conflict on the side of the allies, as indeed they soon did.

Many Americans were pleased, if a trifle frightened. Others were shocked. "The cause of liberty is the cause of man, and neutrality is desertion," H. H. Brackenridge of Kentucky, one of the staunchest Jeffersonians, wrote to George Washington.

But the statement stood. It was the first such declaration in the history of the world, and easily the most important paper to be published by the new government of the United States. It clearly warned the European nations that this country meant to stay out of their quarrels. It could be called the grandfather of the Monroe Doctrine.

★ 5 ★

Citizen Genêt

★ Edmond Charles Édouard Genêt, when he did appear, was a whirlwind. He scintillated. He was bombs bursting in air.

The son of a court official under Louis XVI, he had the gift of tongues, and used it lavishly. He was as much at home in Latin, Swedish, English, or Greek as he was in French, but no matter what language he spoke, his words were fiery; he loved to orate. Despite his family's court connections—and several sisters had been ladies-in-waiting—as soon as the first revolutionists seized power Genêt had embraced their cause, and his demands for *Liberté, Égalité, Fraternité* had been among the loudest in the land.

After his father died, the exuberant lad, barely out of his teens, was sent as a chargé d'affaires to the court of Catherine the Great of Russia. That lady liked his looks, just at first, and she presented him with a pair of highly unrepublican diamond knee buckles, which he wore. Knowing courtiers nodded knowingly, reminding one another, with mnemonic nudges, that such a gift could be followed by an invitation to the royal bedroom. Catherine, however, soon heard of the opinions young Genêt hurled right and left, for this diplomat all his life suffered from a pernicious inability to keep his mouth shut, and, shocked, she sent him home.

This did not check the lad's upswing. In the political reasoning of Paris at the time, to be snubbed by an empress was a proof of fidelity to the cause of the rights of man, so instead of being shelved, he was appointed ambassador to the United States in 1793. He was twenty-nine.

Unexpectedly he arrived not at Philadelphia but at Charleston, several hundred miles down the coast. He *said* that he did this in part because of contrary winds, in part because of a fear that the British navy would intercept him and bring to ruin his philanthropic plans. More likely he did it because there was in Charleston a large body of French émigrés, who had gone there after the slave revolt of August 1791 in Haiti, and who were headed by an energetic consul general, Michel Ange Bernard de Mongourit, who might be useful to the newcomer in his attempt to stir up trouble in the Floridas.

Genêt came in style, aboard the magnificent new French ship *L'Embuscade*. Almost immediately after his landing, he sent this frigate north to Philadelphia without him, for he had elected to make that trip by land—an amazing decision, the roads being what they were.

Charleston made much of Genêt. He was called upon by Gillous, Manigaults, LeGarés, Grimkés. Governor Moultrie fairly fawned upon him. Mangourit hailed him as a deliverer. He made a thrilling appearance—a man of medium height but broadshouldered, with flashing blue eyes, auburn hair, a ruddy complexion. To his fellow countrymen in the New World, he must have seemed the very epitome of the French Revolution, a fearsome figure as he held forth on the glories of the somewhat sanguinary Brotherhood of Man. He never turned down an invitation to speak. He had all sorts of things dedicated to him and was made the honorary president of all sorts of societies.

He found time, however, despite all the speeches, the wreaths, the toasts, and the resolutions, to commission four vessels as

French privateers and to enlist their crews. He created a French admiralty court under Mangourit, to whom he gave funds and blank army commissions to be used to raise an expedition against the Spanish in Florida. He had no right to do these things.

Here was a man with a mission, a man who was about to make over the world. Assuredly he could not be held to ordinary conventional everyday rules of decency and political procedure; nor should he be reminded of these, for the cheers were too loud in his ears to permit him to hear any warning. So, beaming, bowing acknowledgments, accepting bouquets, he bounced from platform to platform, a zealot, a messenger supremely sure of himself, a liberator, a bringer of light.

When, on April 19, after eleven glorious days in Charleston, Genêt started for the capital of the country, it was in a coach drawn by six horses, the gifts of huzzahing admirers. He took twenty-eight days for the trip, or about four times as long as might have been expected. This was because he zigzagged, so as to visit every town or village where there was a colony, howsoever small, of French émigrés, and he continued to give speeches, accept honorary titles, and listen to applause. When he reached Richmond, however, he heard about the President's neutrality proclamation, a terrible jolt, and he called off a scheduled appearance in nearby Fredericksburg in order to proceed directly and hastily to the capital, which he reached on May 16, five weeks and three days after he had landed in America.

All that had gone before was dwarfed by the reception accorded him in Philadelphia. There were parades, bands, speeches, the presentation of colors, all the rest of it, and on a large scale.

Edmond Charles Édouard Genêt had his orders. He had been told there was an active body of pro-French Americans, and he must associate himself with it and lead it. The minister Hamilton, he had been told, was in the pay of the British and would oppose him, but the *foreign* minister, Thomas Jefferson, was France's friend, who would help him in every way possible. Genêt was to consolidate the Gallomen of America. This should

be easy, for they craved a leader, but he was not to bring about
a declaration of war! France preferred a biased neutrality. He
was to do everything to confound Great Britain and also Spain
in the New World, causing them to split their forces. He was, if
possible, to collect some or all of the United States debt to France,
amounting just then to about $2.5 million, though he could ac-
cept payment in grain, which France desperately needed.

These were Genêt's instructions, and he was a conscientious
man. Moreover, the warmth of his reception, all along the line
but most particularly in Philadelphia itself, convinced him that
his superiors back home had been right, and that these men who
cheered him were the *real* American people. Issuance of the
Proclamation of Neutrality had been a crunching blow, but the
ambassador soon convinced himself that it represented the sentiments of only a few effete aristocrats, pitiful leftovers.

He had been warned about Alexander Hamilton, whose scorn did
not disconcert him. Hamilton, even before he met the man, despised Genêt.

The Secretary of State, Citizen Jefferson, was warm, as
expected, but even he shied from the ambassador's bold moves in
the name of the Rights of Man—the issuance of French army
commissions, the encouragement of privateers, the proclamations
sent to Nova Scotia, to Canada, to New Orleans, calling for freedom from the tyranny of Great Britain or of Spain. These things,
Jefferson insisted, were not any ambassador's business.

Genêt's meeting with the President took place in the Deshler
house on May 18, just two days after the ambassador reached
Philadelphia. It was not a warm meeting but Genêt survived.
Nothing could dim his brilliance, nothing diminish his ebullience,
not even the actions of *L'Embuscade,* which, on her way from
Charleston to Philadelphia had picked up various British prizes.
Most of them had been taken on the high seas, but one had been
in United States waters, the lower Delaware Bay.

International law was new, its edges fuzzy, and the whole business of the United States' wartime relations with European na-

tions was bewildering just then, but at least everybody had known that *this* was a crime, and the young British ambassador, George Hammond, had immediately and properly protested.

The French consul general in Philadelphia had been appealed to, but refused to give a judgment. This could wait, he said, until Citizen Genêt, on his way north from Charleston at the time of the incident, arrived in the capital. The matter was put to Genêt even before he had presented his credentials to President Washington, and he grandly and loudly ordered the prize to be returned to her British owners. Genêt's decision was meant to be a gesture of goodwill, and he was irked when the Americans, even Citizen Jefferson, insisted upon regarding it as no more than what a sovereign nation might expect.

The West was the most vulnerable part of this new American nation, the part likeliest to chip off. From the very start there had been mutterings of secession, most of them in New England, a few in Virginia, but in the West these threats never died.

The West was in a seemingly unending state of ferment. It believed that it had been ignored, its needs unnoticed, while at the same time it was obliged to pay taxes like the rich Easterners. On June 1, 1792, Kentucky had been admitted to the Union as the fifteenth state (Vermont, now flirting with British officials in Canada with possible readmission to the empire in mind, had been the fourteenth), and Tennessee was knocking at the door. But the Northwest Territory—all the land north of the Ohio and south of the Great Lakes, comprising the present states of Ohio, Indiana, Illinois, Michigan, and Wisconsin—remained sparsely settled. Such settlers as there were in the Northwest Territory were troubled both by the threat of Indians and by that of the British, who in violation of the treaty that ended the Revolutionary War had refused to give up their military posts at Detroit, Michilimackinac, Fort Erie, Oswego, Oswegatchie on the St. Lawrence, and Pointe-au-Fer and Dutchman's Point on Lake Champlain "with all convenient speed."

These settlers, as well as those who lived south of the Ohio, constantly clamored to know what the central government was going to do about opening and keeping open the mouth of the Mississippi. This entrance-exit, which the Spaniards intermittently threatened to close, was the Westerners' lifeline. Without it they would be cut off from the world, unable to sell what they made and what they grew. The mountains between East and West were such a high barrier, and the roads were so poor where there were any roads at all, that it was cheaper to send a barrel of merchandise from Cincinnati to New York by water—via the Ohio, the Mississippi, the Gulf, and the Atlantic—than by land. Hence, the Westerners were discontented.

Many of the Westerners, it should be remembered—most of the early ones, that is—had been Loyalists, or Tories, at the time of the Revolution, and had crossed the mountains in order to escape persecution at the hands of the American Patriots (rebels to them), so that they had not been favorably disposed toward the central government in the first place. Now Citizen Genêt was sending agents among them to distribute French army commissions and French government funds and to urge an insurrection.

This insurrection would not be directed against the United States as such but rather against the British in Canada (sometimes) or (sometimes) the Spaniards in New Orleans—it all depended upon which side of the Ohio River the hirelings of Edmond Genêt were working. Whichever it was, it could mean the loss of all that part of the world to the United States.

Genêt's men were energetic. They even sought out and sobered up for the occasion the West's favorite military hero, George Rogers Clark, who, though he was a wilderness fighter who had never previously been anything more than a lieutenant-colonel of militia, was now created a major general in the forces of France.

This was intolerable, though it was only the most brash of the ambassador's doings. The situation was made the more awkward by the behavior of the United States ambassador to France, Gouverneur Morris, who was actively working for what was left

of the royalist cause in France. President Washington, asked to
recall him, did so, appointing as his successor the young Virginia
lawyer James Monroe, a devotee of Thomas Jefferson.

Washington was only striving to keep a political balance, divid-
ing the plums as evenly as he could between representatives of
the two schools of constitutional thought, but Monroe proved to
be as embarrassing an envoy as Morris, though in the opposite
direction. Monroe waved the tricolor so vigorously and shouted
revolutionary slogans in such a loud voice that Washington, scan-
dalized, summoned him home.

Hamilton, at Cabinet meetings in Philadelphia, kept asking
for Genêt's recall, while Jefferson, though disappointed in the
whirlwind's behavior, warned that any such reprimand would be
"unkind," for, he pointed out, "friendly nations always negotiate
little differences in private."

What was an infant republic supposed to do in these circumstances? There were no guideposts. The statesmen of Philadelphia
stood on a shaky trestle that might collapse at any misstep.

The ambassador himself was untroubled by talk of a *persona
non grata* action. He was a friend of the People, wasn't he? He
carried out his instructions, didn't he? So Citizen Washington disapproved of his methods? And who, and what, was Washington?
He was an outmoded symbol, a reminder, and an unpleasant
one, of the not dear dead days when lords lorded it over the
plebes, when autocrats, drunk with power, waded ankle deep
in blood to gain their goal. Genêt called George Washington *le
vieillard,* "the Old Man." Any time he thought he needed to,
Genêt said, he could bypass this glittering landmark and appeal
directly to the American people, who would support him. He
really believed this. Of all the mistakes he made, that was the
greatest.

★ 6 ★

A Burnt-Out Comet

★ A new nation is a touchy nation, thin-skinned, jealous of its prerogatives, alert to snap at any slur or to scream at an insult. It was unthinkable that the government of the United States should go on enduring the misbehavior of that jumping jack Genêt. But again, what rights did it have in this matter, what duties? Randolph would vouchsafe no opinion. Jefferson, though he refused actually to *apologize* for Genêt, refused as well to recommend any remedial treatment. Hamilton, however, had an answer.

Put it up to the Supreme Court, said Hamilton.

Here was a solution that appealed to George Washington. This was, after all, a legal problem. He was not sure whether the United States had a right to demand Genêt's recall, or even just to request it, but the Supreme Court should certainly know. The Supreme Court would be, as it were, Washington's council of war.

He and Hamilton got together and framed a set of twenty-nine questions to be asked of Chief Justice John Jay and his two associates. The first twenty-one of these were written by the Secretary of the Treasury, the other eight by the President.

It seemed a good time for such an interrogation. Congress had recessed until December, and the Supreme Court was about to sit, in early July. Chief Justice Jay refused to give an answer

47

alone, but insisted upon waiting until the two associate justices
had taken their places. Even then the Court stalled and bumbled,
obviously embarrassed. At last it said no. Its decision was unan-
imous. It would not rule in this matter; such a ruling, it said, establishing a precedent, would be a usurpation of the Executive
powers by the Judicial branch, contrary to the clear dictate of
the Constitution. It returned the twenty-nine questions to the
President, leaving him right back where he had started.

Hamilton, unable to get a clear-cut recall action from the President, who feared that such a thing would bring about war with
France, turned again in a fit of atrabilious exasperation to the
correspondence columns of the *Gazette of the United States,* a
nationally circulated weekly he had helped to subsidize. As he
had done the previous year against Thomas Jefferson when he
suspected Jefferson of being behind the Congressional resistance
to his fiscal measures, he launched a series of bitter letters against
Citizen Genêt. He signed himself "An American," "Catullus," and
"Scourge," but nobody was fooled, for the Treasury Secretary's in-
cisive style, like his venom, was unmistakable.

It did no good. Journalism in the United States, hardly an
admirable institution at that time, did not even pretend to be
impartial. Long before the politicians themselves had ventured to
do so, the newspaper editors had split into two camps or parties,
and whatever one asserted the other denied. So ferociously did
they fight one another that they had no strength left for opposition to the public enemies, and if they were unconvincing, it was
because each was read by its own kind, who sought not enlightenment but confirmation.

Genêt went right on fitting out French privateers in American
ports, often with largely American crews, always with American
guns, and these ships were snagging English cargo vessels by the
score. Hammond, the British ambassador, went on protesting this
procedure, now at the top of his voice.

Genêt's insurrection plans wobbled, however. Except for the
French colony in Charleston, Consul Mongourit could rally little
support for an invasion of the Floridas, and John Buckskin of

Kentucky, though willing to be taken downriver for an attack on New Orleans, not unnaturally thought that he ought to be paid first. Paris, where the political scene was changing once again, denied Genêt more money.

The ambassador, all unabashed, appealed to the Secretary of the Treasury of the United States, asking for debt payments in advance. Hamilton was hardly a laughing man, but he must have come close to a laugh when he read this request. However, he said "no" in a quiet voice, his face flat.

Genêt carried on, all the same. One of the most irritating things about this man was the rudeness with which he answered polite reminders that he was overstepping his station. When a letter produced by two of Hamilton's closest associates, Rufus King and John Jay, seemed to prove that Genêt was indeed threatening to go over the head of George Washington and take his case directly to the American people, Genêt brusquely denied it in a letter addressed to the President. Jefferson himself called the ambassador on this indiscretion:

I am desired to observe to you that it is not the established course for the diplomatic characters residing here, to have any direct correspondence with him. The Secretary of State is the organ through which their communications should pass. The President does not conceive it to be within the line of propriety or duty for him to bear evidence against a declaration which, whether made to him or others, is perhaps immaterial: he therefore declines interfering in the case.

Genêt's answer was a snarl.

At last it was agreed in the Cabinet, even Thomas Jefferson concurring, that the man must go. He was formally notified that the United States government was about to request the French government to recall him. Meanwhile, he was told, he would still be considered the ambassador of the Republic of France. The matter might take several months, because the United States government was not issuing a peremptory demand! It was sending a special envoy to Paris to explain, lest the matter be considered a *casus belli*. The pugnacious French were declaring war on nearly everybody in sight, on almost any pretext, and the statesmen in Philadelphia wanted no war.

At about this time the Black Vomit reared its ugly—and malodorous—head. It must have been the world's *stinkingest* disease, as hard on the nurses as on the patients, hard even on the neighbors. It hit suddenly, with no warning, the seemingly healthy victim keeling over with a groan, helpless thereafter. The temperature rose frightfully and rapidly. The skin turned yellow and was very dry. The coated tongue was a dirty-white. The eyes were glazed. The breath was foul, and this, together with the fact that defecation and urination were almost continuous and were uncontrollable, accounted for the stench. Men said that it was enough to take the paint off the walls.

The patient suffered horribly. The climax came on the fourth or fifth day, and if the patient survived—though few did—he recovered, though much debilitated.

In Philadelphia, where it was believed, probably correctly, that it came from the West Indies, this ailment was usually called the Islands Fever or the Santo Domingo Fever, though some called it the name by which it was later generally known, from the color it turned the skin, the Yellow Fever. The Spaniards called it *el vomito negro,* an accurate description.

The most horrible thing about this visitation was its mysterious nature. Nobody knew what caused it, where it came from. Nobody knew how to prevent its spread, much less how to stamp it out. The people of Philadelphia, that center of science and the arts, were in a panic. They tried Jesuits' Bark, ipecacuanha, pitiny tea, and Delaney's Aromatic Distilled Vinegar. They fired cannons in the streets, there being a common belief that this would burn off the "vapors" that caused the fever, and they built bonfires.

September 6 Dr. James Hutchinson, one of the most respected physicians in the city, died of the Black Vomit. Two days later, the worst day yet, there were forty-two deaths, a week after that, forty-eight. The gravediggers could not bury them fast enough, and the ringing of the passing-bell, a church bell that signaled another death, was forbidden. On September 24 there were ninety-six deaths. And it continued to grow worse.

People refused to shake hands, even with their best friends. When they had to go out-of-doors, they walked in the middle of the street, keeping as far from all houses as possible. They spread fresh earth two inches deep on the floors of their houses. They carried pieces of tarred rope and hung camphor bags around their necks; they took baths of myrrh and black pepper. They also prayed.

It was assumed that the Islands Fever came from some tropical place, though it had been known to strike in force as far north as Halifax, Nova Scotia, and this was not its first descent upon Philadelphia, though it was by far the worst.

Some blamed it on the weather, which had been uncommonly dry and warm. Others attributed it to the large number of Benjamin Franklin's lightning rods that had been erected in the city, which rods, "by imperceptibly drawing the electric fluid from the clouds," rendered the town predisposed to the plague. One anonymous faddist wrote in a newspaper that mosquitoes might be the carrying agent, but nobody paid any attention to him.

It was a shattering experience. In the two and a half months that the epidemic raged, more than four thousand persons died. Everybody who could do so went away, and Philadelphia, the most populous city in the New World, was a ghost town. The whole business, it was estimated, cost the city the staggering sum of $2 million.

Oddly, politics, which had become one of Philadelphia's biggest businesses, was little affected. The business of national government was at a standstill, but it usually stood still at that time of the year anyway. Congress had adjourned on schedule just before the outbreak in the third week in August, and the Congressmen returned, gingerly enough, late in November after the epidemic had run its course. President Washington, early in that terrible time, had left for Mount Vernon, where he was to stay until the reassembling of Congress, but this had been his custom and was not remarked upon. Thomas Jefferson, some time before, had rented a pleasant house on the Schuylkill River near Gray's Ferry, and there he sat it out, entertaining friends from time to time and now and then sending into the city to ask about the newly invented threshing machine he had ordered from Scotland. The machine was overdue, and he was worried about it. He was only getting eight bushels of wheat an acre, and that wasn't enough.

Alexander Hamilton, however, almost made himself into a martyr. He too had rented a house in the country, though his was only about two miles out, and he went into town almost every day, being, as always, in a fury of work. He came down early with a particularly virulent case of the Islands Fever, and for several days his life hung by a thread. His wife, too, was stricken, though not so severely, while their four children, who were with them, escaped unscathed.

The Secretary of the Treasury did not call in the distinguished hero of the plague, Dr. Benjamin Rush, but rather a younger Philadelphia physician, one who deplored Rush's practice of purging and bloodletting, Dr. Edward Stevens. It is likely that this choice was made not because Rush was a fervent Jeffersonian, but rather because Stevens was Hamilton's boyhood friend from the sugar islands. Stevens prescribed infusions of bark and a series of cold baths for both Mr. and Mrs. Hamilton, and soon, shaken, much weakened, they were to make their way to the home of her parents in Albany, New York, to recuperate. It was late in October before the Secretary of the Treasury got back on the job.

Edmond Charles Édouard Genêt, too, weathered the storm, though he had spent much of the time in New York, where he was called to help quell a mutiny in the French fleet that had lately put in from Martinique, an occasion that did his cause no good.

When word came from Paris about the government's recall request, Genêt might well have wished for a moment that he *had* been taken. In France the Girondists, of which he was one, had been overthrown by the Jacobins, a much more bloodthirsty group.

The Jacobins did not like Citizen Genêt, whom they found guilty of "criminal manoeuvres," and they asked the Secretary of State in Philadelphia to please send him back; they were dispatching a successor, Jean Antoine Joseph Fauchet.

"A burnt-out comet," Alexander Hamilton called Genêt.

Genêt thought fast. He knew what the Jacobins wanted: They wanted his head, literally. He swallowed his pride and asked President Washington, *le vieillard,* for political asylum. He was the first person ever to do so.

Washington granted the request. There is no written record, but it seems certain that the President extracted a preliminary promise that Genêt, if allowed to remain in America, would never take part in politics again. At any rate, he never did. He became a United States citizen, and married well—Cornelia Tappen Clinton, daughter of the governor of New York. He settled down as a gentleman farmer on Long Island and later in Rensselaer County, New York, where he lived until 1834, dying on July 14—Bastille Day.

★ 7 ★

The Amenities of Wave Ruling

★ It was as though the baby nation had been born in a thunderstorm. The crashes were almost continuous. The gods never ceased to roar. No sooner had Edmond Charles Édouard Genêt been cleared out of the way than there loomed ahead the many-tentacled enormity of Great Britain. *Something* had to be done about the British, or the United States would find itself at war again.

The Americans had many complaints against them: their retention of the western wilderness forts; their impressment of American seamen; their incitement of the Indians in the Northwest Territory; and their extraordinary harassment of American commerce while they were at war with France.

Britannia ruled the waves, and she wanted everybody to know it. She ruled them with a scowling jealousy that suggested she feared somebody meant to take them away.

When the Mediterranean was the whole world, when "long ships" were largely oar-propelled, naval tactics had been based on the assumption that a sailing vessel was essentially a transport, an instrument used by the army, not in itself an engine of war. Many galleys did mount rams, true, but these were seldom used except as threats and in out-of-fleet duels, for disengagement after the ramming of even a small vessel could take time. During that time the rammer was vulnerable to other enemy ships from both sides and astern at the same time. The accepted tactic was to grapple and board. In other words, a sea fight was a land fight that happened to take place afloat, and the successful admiral was the one who could get alongside first with the most men.

Even after seamen had ventured beyond the Pillars of Hercules into the vast reaches of the Atlantic, and the "long ship" of war had been replaced by the "round ship" of war, fighting vessels remained essentially military transports, their guns no more than accessories. The Spanish Armada had been designed and built to carry an army to England, and what cannons and gunpowder and ball it carried were meant for land use and stowed so far below on those overcrowded ships—overcrowded with soldiers and their arms and effects—that they could not be brought up and put to use in time to do any good. The English vessels were smaller and faster than the Spanish ships. They sailed circles around them, peppering them at long distance, damaging their rudders and their running gear. They defeated the Spaniards by staying away from them, in defiance of all the accepted rules of battle, while Spanish soldiers lined the gunwales and shook their fists and screamed at the dastardly English mariners, daring them to come up close and fight like men. "We will pluck them feather by feather," gloated the English admiral, Howard of Effingham, and this, the weather aiding, is pretty much what happened.

The English had perfected this technique. They had made a tradition of it, revolutionizing warfare at sea. They developed their navy into a full-time, all-purpose machine, until by the eighteenth century it outnumbered, outgunned, and outweighed all of the others put together.

Such a navy was expensive. As commerce multiplied, as the world got larger with the discovery of America and the opening up of the Indies West and East, as piracy increased, more and bigger warships were called for. These ships had to be high-sided overall, not just at the fore- and aftercastles, and they had more decks and mounted many more guns. As the manufacture of powder and the founding of cannon improved, the pieces became heavier, perforce, and the balls were heavier too. The ships had to be beamy, in order to stay upright at a broadside, and this meant that they had to be longer, and the sticks had to be taller, carrying more canvas.

The Anglomen in America had repeatedly assured President Washington that England did not really mean all those growled warnings to neutrals that she gave forth in the name of her navy, but the Anglomen were taken aback and fell silent when the British navy, faced with the problem of subduing a fanatical and unpredictable France, proclaimed that whole nation to be in a state of blockade. The result—one result—was to choke American trade. The British included the French West Indies in this blockade, and a great deal of the American trade was carried on with the Indies.

When Great Britain renegotiated her treaty with Portugal, she released Portugal from the duty of blocking the Strait of Gibraltar against Algerian pirates, who until that time had been confined to the Mediterranean Sea. This was done in order to release Portuguese ships for duty in the blockade against France, but to Americans it looked like a deal with the pirates, who thereupon poured out into the Atlantic, where they captured dozens of American merchant vessels, selling the crews into slavery. The United States was the only nation with ships in those parts that had not agreed to pay regular blackmail to Algeria, Tunis, Morocco, and Tripoli. The United States couldn't afford it.

On November 6, 1793, a British order in council authorized the seizure of neutral vessels carrying anything to or from any French island anywhere. This was bad enough, but no announcement of the issuance of the order was made, excepting to warship captains, until late in December. By that time the bag was about 150 ships, almost all of them American.

This tactic was considered a legitimate *ruse de guerre*. British naval officers at that time were extraordinarily touchy, and duels were frequent, but the concept of professional honor never seemed even to have brushed the Admiralty itself. It countenanced and even encouraged all sorts of dirty tricks. For instance, on December 20, 1780, near the end of the American Revolution, Great Britain suddenly and secretly declared war on the United Netherlands. A fast dispatch boat was sent to Jamaica to inform Admiral Rodney of this fact and to instruct him to descend upon everything Dutch, beginning, specifically, with St. Eustatius, "the Golden Rock," an open port through which most of the gunpowder used by the American Continental army was transshipped. At the Rock the Dutch had been given no warning. Only with the arrival of Rodney's fleet, on February 3, 1781, did they learn that war had been declared. The town fell without a shot, and that included all the shipping in the roads, almost two hundred sail. What's more, Rodney did not run up a British flag afterward, but kept the Dutch flag flying over Fort Oranje. Through the weeks that followed scores of other vessels, their skippers not having heard about the declaration of war, put in at St. Eustatius, and were snapped up. Rodney, a bankrupt gambler, not only was not punished for this: he was given a large share of the loot and raised to the peerage.

It might be thought that with the acceptance of the United States as an independent nation the impressment of seamen at least would fade away, but it continued. Impressment, by both the army and the navy, was as old as England.

In their context, the noun and verb "press" have nothing to do with the press of work or the pressing of a pair of pants, but stem from the medieval French *preste,* the modern *prête,* meaning "ready." The man who accepted a "preste," or symbol of readiness to serve his sovereign—always, in England, this symbol was a shilling piece, the "King's [or Queen's] shilling"—was taken to have made a solemn vow, The fact that the coin had been slipped into his hand while he lay dead drunk under a tavern table, or after he had been hit on the head for insisting that he *wasn't* ready, made no difference. The navy needed men. The army could get fillers, when shorthanded, from three different sources: from the jails; from Ireland, which was always starving; and after the various Stuart uprisings, and in particular after that of the Young Pretender in 1745, from the Highlands of Scotland.

These areas were not suitable recruiting places for the navy, which insisted that it needed *trained* men, and more and more of them.

Conditions in the Royal Navy being what they were—the quarters filthy, the pay miniscule, the food unspeakable, the punishments appallingly brutal—desertion flourished. The seamen quit in droves, though hanging could be the punishment if they were caught. It was to recover these deserters and put them back to work that the press-gangs were sent out, or at least, so the Royal Navy said. The bully boys swept grog shops and brothels indiscriminately, enslaving any able-bodied man who even looked like a sailor and could speak English. If such a man should object that he was an American and should offer to prove it by calling in his captain to identify him, the cudgelmen took him along anyway. He was probably lying, probably a deserter.

The United States authorities issued citizenship papers to mariners who could prove that they had been born in America or had been naturalized there, but British pressers tore them up, declaring that they were forgeries, as indeed many of them were. Anyway, in British eyes no man could "become" a citizen of another nation. The official belief was "Once an Englishman, always an Englishman." This was known as the Doctrine of Indefeasible Allegiance.

When the pressers couldn't find all the "recruits" they needed in the ports, they found them on the high seas, stopping all merchant vessels, many of which, of course, were American.

The situation was bad, and now that England was at war with France, it was sure to get worse.

The matter of the wilderness forts posed an even more immediate threat to the peace and continued existence of the United States.

Nobody on either side of the sea even pretended that Detroit, Michilimackinac, Dutchman's Point, and the others were not in territory acknowledged to be a part of the United States by the Treaty of Paris of 1783. The British had kept them, fully garrisoned, as a guarantee against the debts the various states owed to British merchants, or so they said, but this was probably an afterthought. Americans in general believed that the forts were retained because Britain still hoped to maintain the Great Indian Neutral Ground she had dreamed about for years, protecting the Indians in that part of the world and at the same time making friends with them. They could thus keep American settlers out while establishing a jumping-off station for a possible future expedition from Canada to the lower Mississippi country and the two Floridas.

If this should happen—and it was hard to see how anything short of war could prevent it—the British would hem in the new republic from the west and the south, as already, with Canada, they hemmed it in from the north. The Royal Navy of course would take care of the east. The noble American experiment could not be expected to withstand the pressure of such a vise. It would vanish like the flame of a whuffed-out candle.

The British Foreign Office was always aware, too, of the influence that the control of so many western Indians would have over the semistate of Vermont, with which they were dickering over a separate peace treaty, and which they still hoped to annex to Canada. Also, there was the fur trade. This represented half a million dollars a year, and it was growing. So long as there were redcoats stationed in the Northwest Territory, the furs would go down the St. Lawrence to the sea and eventually reach England. If those redcoats were withdrawn, the Indians would ship this product down the Mohawk and the Hudson, United States streams.

It was always possible, too, that the Kentuckians and Tennesseeans, disgusted with what was happening in Philadelphia, would organize their own expedition against New Orleans, first making a deal with the British in Canada in order to protect their own rear. Genêt's aborted plan was not the only one of its sort, just the noisiest. The shooting might start any day.

The governor general of Canada was a reasonable man, a sensible man, who recently had visited London to confer with his superiors. He had been Sir Guy Carleton and was now Lord Dorchester. On his return to the wilderness he had a long talk with the lieutenant governor, John G. Simcoe, another military man. Simcoe despised George Washington. His most fervent hope was that he might have a chance to measure swords with Washington on the field. He believed that a "preventive war" was needed, and the wonder was that he had not brought it about single-handed while he was acting governor of the province.

No doubt it was on Simcoe's advice that Lord Dorchester built a new fort on the Maumee sixty miles southwest of Detroit. This was deep in United States territory, and the construction in itself could be taken as an act of war. At one point, indeed, the red-coats there faced a large part of the United States Army under General "Mad Anthony" Wayne. Wayne, however, did not live up to his nickname. He was cautious. After a confabulation with the British commanding officer, he withdrew his troops. But it had been a near thing.

Dorchester went further. On February 10, 1794, addressing a large and supposedly representative gathering of Northwest Territory Indians, he warned them that the United States and Great Britain would soon be at war, the clear implication being that if they, the Indians, started it they would not be blamed. Dorchester had meant that news of this speech, delivered deep in the wilderness, should not leak out, but it did leak out, causing consternation on both sides of the mountains. In Philadelphia it precipitated an embargo movement aimed at England, a movement that failed to get through Congress only because of the tie-breaking vote of the Vice President, John Adams.

Things were coming to a head.

★ 8 ★

An Honest Man Sent Abroad

★ In Philadelphia a small group of high-flight Anglomen—or Federalists, as they were beginning to call themselves—huddled for a discussion of this crisis. Most of them were Senators. All were distinguished. They agreed that the United States, despite previous disappointments with John Adams and Gouverneur Morris, should send to England an ambassador armed with extraordinary powers and authorized to assemble a treaty. The group further decided that Alexander Hamilton was the man for this job, and that Senator Oliver Ellsworth of Connecticut should so notify President Washington.

The wonder here is that Hamilton consented to such a gathering. He was not a committee man, a conferencer; customarily he acted alone. Jefferson had quit the government, and the Cabinet meetings were now one-man shows. Why didn't the Secretary of the Treasury put himself forward on such an occasion?

The only explanation that is reasonable is that Hamilton had overexerted his influence with the President, who, always thin-skinned, feared that people might be calling him weak. The President missed Jefferson. He could hardly have known that people were calling the Secretary of the Treasury an *éminence grise,* the power behind the throne, but he might have suspected this, and would certainly have resented it.

Washington had not wanted the Presidency in the first place, and when his original term of office was nearing an end, he had asked James Madison to write for him a farewell address to be given to the American people. Madison did this, but the thing had gone unused after the President's friends, Jefferson and Hamilton prominent among them, convinced him that unless he accepted a second term the government might collapse. Yet as soon as he had started upon that second term, the newspapers, or some of them, began to criticize his leadership. This troubled him.

On March 10, 1794, at the Deshler house, Ellsworth presented the proposal of a special envoy to England, and the President instantly agreed. But when Senator Ellsworth went on to say that he and his friends had voted that Secretary Hamilton would make the best possible man for the post, George Washington demurred. Secretary Hamilton, the President said, lacked the confidence of the people. That was certainly true, but it was strange that George Washington should know it—and admit it.

The Secretary of the Treasury had put through his financial system, almost complete, against stiff opposition, and he was now prepared to follow Jefferson out of the Cabinet. Again and again he had seemed to be cornered, but with report after brilliant report he had cleared himself and left his enemies cursing in bafflement. The reports, classics now, had all been in writing. Hamilton had wished to report to the Congress in person, the way they did it in England, but Congress had vetoed this. The written arrangement, though he resented it, had worked out to Hamilton's advantage. He was a poor speaker but a clear, persuasive writer.

The Secretary's figures were irrefutable, his facts rocks. And yet the man in the street simply could not believe that a $1,200-a-year official with no private means could set up a $10-million national bank calculated to make so many rich men richer, and could impose heavy taxes upon the people, without letting some of the stuff stick to his own fingers. It was all there on paper, all accounted for. The Secretary, it would seem, was incorrigibly honest, even though many of his friends weren't. But the public still shook a dubious head.

So Washington said no to Oliver Ellsworth, who had to go back to his compatriots with this word.

Washington, however, still thought that a special envoy would be a good idea, and after some thought he appointed John Jay.

At a glance this seemed a good choice. Jay, a New York lawyer, was intensely conservative. Though of French and Dutch extraction, he hated all things French, and at the same time he was an admirer of the English. His patriotism and integrity were unquestioned. Dry, caustic, stick-brittle, he was a learned man who had served his country carefully and well, first in Spain, then in England. He had been one of that group of wonder-workers—Benjamin Franklin, John Adams, William Pinckney were the others—who had put through the Treaty of Paris in 1783, a stunning American victory.

Yet there were objections, and rude persons raised them immediately. For one thing, John Jay happened to be the Chief Justice of the United States Supreme Court, and there were many who believed that it would not be wise—even if it was legal—for him to serve in a diplomatic post at the same time.

The Westerners were especially wrought up. Would such a functionary make a good ambassador? To them the whole purpose of a parley with Great Britain was to get the redcoats removed from the wilderness forts, thus eliminating the threat of a British advance upon New Orleans. The Westerners believed that the federal government had let them down when it did not insist upon an unconditional, permanent pledge to open the Mississippi for all time. Jay was the worst of those effete Easterners who sought to sell out the settlers of the West for the benefit of a few New England traders. Hadn't he, as chairman of the Foreign Relations Committee under the old Articles of Confederation—as, in effect, the pre-Jefferson Secretary of State—hadn't he virtually conceded to Spain the unqualified right to seal the mouth of the Mississippi in return for certain small commercial advantages that could benefit only his rich friends? He was a traitor! When the appointment was announced, the West exploded in rage. Resolutions of protest poured in upon the government in Philadelphia.

The passing of resolutions of a political nature, often fiery in their wording, was one way for early American citizens to express themselves. Letters to newspapers were of course another, but these were limited to the cities, where few Americans lived. The resolutions, on the other hand, might be adopted at mass meetings open to the public or at meetings of discussion clubs.

The discussion clubs had been started in Philadelphia early in the year 1793 and within a short time had spread to every state but Georgia. They were unofficial and, theoretically, nonpartisan. Their birth seems to have been spontaneous. Because so many of them appeared at the time when Genêt was making his big splash on the national scene, they were sometimes called, by those who didn't like them, Jacobin Clubs. In fact they had no connection with the Jacobin Clubs of the French Revolution, and though Genêt might have accepted an honorary presidency here and there, he never started a club or inspired its organization.

They were generally called Democratic Clubs, and that is odd, because "democratic" was a dirty word of that period, when even the most outspoken opponents of the central government preferred to call themselves Republicans. The government adherents were known as Federalists. Both of these were misnomers, for the Federalists were in favor of a strong republican form of government, whereas the Republicans—or Democrats, as eventually they came to be called—were accused by the Federalists of being slanted toward the old loose Articles of Confederation.

The Democratic Clubs—"Demoniacal clubs" the Federalists dubbed them—were generally county organizations, their interests parochial. There was nothing secret about them. They had no central control, and they did not correspond much with one another. Most of them elected their own officers fresh every year, sometimes every month. Though professing to be nonpolitical, they were largely liberal—that is, critical of the government—in their views.

The Federalists, "the wise, the well-born, and the rich," in the words of their high priest Theodore Sedgwick, had their own clubs, exclusive groups that did not need to stoop to the vulgarity of the mass meeting. To them the members of the Democratic Clubs were "the jackals of Mobocracy." They abhorred and feared them, and as much as possible pushed them away. They approved of the discrimination shown by Supreme Court Justice Chase—all of the judges were Federalists, without exception— when he instructed a bailiff to strike from a jury panel the names of "any of those creatures or persons called democrats."

Nevertheless, the clubs, all unabashed, liked to pass resolutions of protest, and to send them to Philadelphia. Washington probably read them, though they roiled him, but he would not be pushed around; he stuck to his nomination of John Jay.

Hamilton, though he did not get the appointment, continued to be the sponsor of the plan. It was he who wrote Jay's instructions.

The man who had taken Jefferson's place as Secretary of State, having been moved up from the Attorney Generalship, was Edmund Randolph. It had been Jefferson's policy to keep international discussions open at both ends, so that he could balance France against Great Britain, Britain against France, taking every advantage that a policy of neutrality could offer to the United States. Randolph proposed to continue this policy.

Not Hamilton! Hamilton was for throwing in with Great Britain in the hope of getting a commercial treaty. He had been treating with British representatives, unofficially, for years and had come to the first Cabinet meeting after the appointment of Jay with a full set of instructions for the new ambassador. He was furious when Randolph pointed out that *he,* after all, was the Secretary of State. Hamilton set the man straight. Waggling an admonitory forefinger, and speaking with the weary patience of one who explains the obvious to the half-witted, Hamilton lectured Randolph at length, reducing him, almost, to silence. Randolph was permitted to insert a few minor clauses into the instructions, but everybody knew that this was done merely to save face, *Randolph*'s face.

John Jay sailed from New York on May 12 amid shouts of encouragement, though there were some boos and catcalls too. Later, the cheerers, the representatives of the wise, the well-born, and the rich, returned to Philadelphia. It would be months, they knew, before they would hear anything from the ambassador, but there was plenty to keep them busy in the meanwhile, for they were faced with a war right in their own country—the Whiskey Insurrection.

★ 9 ★

The Bluster of the Whiskey Boys

★ All the world was waiting for the United States to fall apart. The statesmen in Philadelphia feared this too. The belief persisted that even a small republic was a chancy experiment, while a large one would be self-defeating by its very nature. True, the United States was hanging on somehow, and the spectacular example of France still stood there to dazzle men's eyes. It was also true that while they were still lopping off heads in France—Robespierre's went on July 28—they continued to win victories in the field.

Just the same, persons of probity on both sides of the sea were firm in their belief that kingship, the "natural" form of political organization, soon would be forced back upon the chastened French, and all would be well again. The knowing ones, therefore, peered eagerly every time a rift showed upon the surface of the new American nation as well.

There were many such.

From the beginning the colonies had snarled at one another, squabbling sometimes about boundaries, sometimes about trade. Men in Massachusetts and Connecticut deplored the Rhode Islanders' practice of admitting all sorts of weird religious fanatics —Catholics, Baptists, even Jews. New Jerseyites clucked their tongues and shook their heads over the madhouse that was their neighbor, Pennsylvania, where Mennonites, Moravians, Amish, and other foreign freaks were granted citizenship privileges just as though they were Americans. Southerners were shocked by the New Englanders' "levelling" practices.

Daniel Shays's brush fire in 1786–1787, before the adoption of the Constitution, before a real central government existed, had been the result of another regional misunderstanding. The poor farmers of western Massachusetts had contended that they were underrepresented and overtaxed by the Bostonians and their like. Shays's rebellion had been put down, bloodlessly, by the Massachusetts militia, but it is noteworthy that a part of the New York militia stood by in case it was needed.

Even after they had fought a long war together and the colonies had become states, they quarreled. Virginia and Maryland had long-standing boundary disputes with Pennsylvania, as well as one with each other. Connecticut actually sent militiamen into Pennsylvania, to protect its so-called rights to the Wyoming Valley. New York and New Hampshire again and again approached a full-scale shooting match over Vermont, which both claimed. Disintegration, it might be said, was in the air.

The most conspicuous split, from the beginning, was the North–South one. Here were predestined enemies. Neither side ever made an effort to understand the other, and the differences were loud. In order that the war might be fought, it was of course necessary that the New Englanders, "the Wise Men of the East," who had been running things revolutionary, consent to the appointment of a Virginian, or at least a Southerner of some sort, as commander in chief of the Continental Army. After that, and after the Articles of Confederation had outlived their usefulness and the Constitution had been adopted, Washington was the inevitable choice for President, but it was just as clear that the Vice President, to offset this, must be a Massachusetts man— John Adams, as it happened.

It is remarkable that when North and South at last agreed

upon a site for the capital more or less between the two areas, and the Capitol building itself was being raised, two kinds of stone were used, Massachusetts marble and Virginia sandstone, and each side jealously watched the other to make sure that it did not get in more than its share.

To the North–South rift the statesmen had become attuned. They took it into consideration when they framed laws or imposed taxes. They studied it, fearful that it might grow to perilous proportions, even to war, as indeed eventually it did. Jefferson told Washington in 1792 when he was urging him to run for a second term, "North and South will hang together if they have you to hang on."

Hamilton, when he was pushing his national bank bill through Congress, and issuing reports right and left in the hope of bolstering it, was acutely aware of the South's opposition to banks in general, and did everything that he could to circumvent it. Of the 20 votes against the bill in the House, finally, 15 were from the South, and one prominent Southern Congressman was wont to assert with a snort that he would as soon be seen going into a whorehouse as going into a bank.

The East–West rift, on the other hand, caught the statesmen by surprise. But it shouldn't have. There had been ample warning, because, properly, this split was not new. The colonials had known it earlier. Ever since the first settlers moved back a little from the coast, North, South, or in-between, there had been complaints along the frontier. Taxes were too high; representation in the legislature was unfair; the capital was too far away, and so were the courts. This discontent, which was continuous, often erupted in small acts of violence, and at least once, in the case of the Regulator movement in North Carolina, opposition to taxes imposed by the planter government led to a bloody battle at Alamance Creek in 1771. A series of trials and group hangings followed, but the mountain men, though quieter for a while, still grumbled.

In two of *The Federalist* papers, both of them written by Hamilton, Americans had been virtually promised that under the new constitution no land or excise tax would be levied.

"The genius of the people will ill brook the inquisitive and peremptory spirit of excise laws," Hamilton wrote in Number 12.

And in Number 21: "It is a signal advantage of taxes on articles of consumption, that they contain in their own nature a security against excess. . . . If duties are too high they lessen the consumption—the collection is eluded; and the product to the treasury is not so great as when they are confined within proper and moderate bounds."

But Hamilton's bank was bound to be expensive, the way he had set it up, and even after he had won his beloved protectionist tax on imports he found that he could not raise all the pump-priming money he needed without endangering another of his plans, a commercial treaty with Great Britain. So the barriers were broken down. The revenue agent was let loose upon the land. And citizens, even as they squealed in pain, took to quoting a popular newspaper verse:

> "Each day a fresh report he broaches,
> That spies and nobs may ride in coaches.
> Soldiers and farmers, don't despair;
> Untax'd as yet are—Earth and Air!"

A tax on air and earth would have been bad enough, in all conscience, but one on whiskey, to many, was worse. Eight and a half cents a gallon meant, simply, ruin.

The trouble started in western Pennsylvania, in what is now somewhat grandly called the Golden Triangle, the country bounded by the Monongahela, Allegheny, and Youghiogheny rivers where they come together to form the Ohio. The fast-growing trading post at this place was called Pittsburgh. Discontent soon spilled beyond this region, to embrace the counties of Washington, Allegheny, Fayette, and Westmoreland, also, to some extent, Ohio County, Virginia (today a part of West Virginia).

This territory contained about 1/70th of the population of the

United States. Most of the people were Scots or Scotch-Irish, and they had been brought up on tales of the wickedness of the tax collector. They were hardheaded, grim, touchy, tough.

They lived, these men, in country that was to become famous for its production of coal, centered by a city that was to become the greatest maker of steel in all the world, but such achievements were beyond their dreams in the late eighteenth century. The only thing that they produced in any quantity then, the only crop that they could depend upon, was grain, mostly rye. And for the sternest economic reasons the form that this grain took for them was whiskey.

To say that whiskey was their life blood would be physiologically inaccurate but poetically sound. Their livelihood was dictated by their geographical position, something that the grabby, greedy Easterners never seemed to get into their heads. The hillbillies were halfway over the mountains, so to speak. They were many miles short of the fine open fields of Kentucky and Ohio, yet they had left the lowlands of Pennsylvania far behind. What they grew they must either ship down the great rivers, the Ohio, the Mississippi, or send back over almost unbelievably rocky roads to the East—after, of course, they had eaten and drunk as much of it as they could.

The long river route beckoned, despite the many weeks and months that the trip would take. There was plenty of timber in the Pittsburgh neighborhood, so that boats and rafts could be built. But who could be sure that the southern gateway would remain open? And of course no return from the product was possible if the Spaniards, capricious and corrupt as they were, had closed the river at New Orleans. So the grain, perforce, went eastward.

A horse—and horses were expensive in those parts, where there were no mules—could carry only four bushels of grain. but *twenty-four* bushels of rye could be transformed into sixteen gallons of whiskey, and a horse could easily tote that by carrying an eight-gallon keg on each side. The stills themselves cost little; any hillbilly could make and operate one. There were about

1,200 stills in the Golden Triangle district, a quarter of all the stills in the nation, most of the others being used for the rendering of rum out of molasses imported from the French West Indies.

So whiskey was money in Appalachia, where there was no cash. It was the people's way of life. That is why, when the federal government proposed to tax it, the Whiskey Boys set up a howl. They kept saying that they couldn't possibly pay the whiskey tax, even if they were willing to do so, for they had no money. They lived largely by barter, but the men in the East paid no attention to this.

The Whiskey Boys had no accepted leader or group of leaders. They never pledged themselves to one code of conduct, and they never, in so many words or by any action, *defied* the central government. They held mass meetings, and, as was the custom, they passed resolutions petitioning Philadelphia for relief.

They built no forts, stocked no magazines. They had no form of military organization, not even a cadre. They made many fiery speeches, but no real demand. Off the record, they would admit that they were pinning their hopes on two beliefs: one, that the regular army, a handful of ragamuffins scattered throughout the Northwest Territory, where they were desperately needed to face up to the redcoats and Indians in those six wilderness strongholds, would not be used against them; and two, that the Pennsylvania militia, knowing what a tough nut their mountain position would be to crack, would refuse such a service. They themselves never entertained any thought of attacking anyone.

There were isolated outrages. Two tax collectors, at different times, were set upon, beaten, and hot-tarred. A post rider was held up, and the mail he carried was rifled in the hope of learning the plans, if any, of the men in Philadelphia.

The chief excise inspector for western Pennsylvania, John Neville, had got rich by speculating in Mr. Hamilton's funded debt securities, at the expense of many a poor farmer and war veteran. He would have been hated anyway, in that position, and when his house was burned down and one of his aides was killed—apparently by a stray shot—it was put down by the Whiskey Boys as little more than a routine disturbance out on that turbulent frontier.

What the Whiskey Boys did not realize was that in Philadelphia all these matters loomed very large. Today the air-line distance between Pittsburgh and Philadelphia is 254 miles, but by the old roads the distance must have been well over 300 miles, and the stories were retold many times in the course of that journey, increasing in gaudiness with each time.

The Federalists, and especially the so-called High Federalists or followers of Hamilton, were frightened. They cried bloody murder; they cried black treason. They blamed the most convenient bogeyman they could find, the sundry Democratic Clubs scattered across the country. The clubs, they said, had been paid by the French revolutionary atheists to do just this—to split the country in half.

There were only three such clubs in the district involved, and only one of them, the Washington County Democratic Club—popularly, the Mingo Creek Club—had made any protest about the tax on whiskey. But the High Federalists did not know this, or ignored it. The Federalists called for an army to put down these rebels, to prevent them from holding mass meetings and from passing resolutions.

When the Federalists did this they turned their backs on the Constitution, the first Amendment of which reads that "Congress shall make no law . . . abridging . . . the right of the people peaceably to assemble, and to petition the Government for a redress of grievances."

Hamilton has been blamed for this outcry against the Democratic Clubs, for it was known that he favored a large standing army, which he hoped some day to lead, and of course it was he who had brought the whiskey tax into being in the first place. But even some conservative Republicans joined in the cry, and in the Cabinet the loudest voice against the club movement was that of the former Attorney General, now Secretary of State, Jefferson's successor, Edmund Randolph. Washington too seems to have suspected the clubs of dark doings long before the Whiskey Insurrection, for he always tied them in his mind to Citizen Genêt.

Not that Hamilton was silent! He was much too intelligent to credit the wild stories that came out of the West, but he knew a threat to his financial system when he saw one. Here was a direct confrontation of the masses, the states, with the federal government. Petty or not, this revolt, if it was a revolt, and even if it was not, must be put down, and it must be done emphatically, immediately, and in overwhelming force.

He had a plan. He always had a plan. Granted, the full-time professional army was tied up in the wilderness, but the militia could be used, and not just the Pennsylvania militia—Governor Mifflin already had declared that he didn't believe this organization could do the job—but the militia from New Jersey and Maryland and Virginia as well. They were all interested, or should be.

The President should take command in person, Hamilton said. He should take the field. Washington, who was sixty-two, agreed.

Orders went out to the four governors on August 17. There would be 12,950 soldiers in all, 11,000 infantry, 1,500 cavalry, 450 artillery. The New Jersey and Pennsylvania militias should rendezvous at Carlisle, Pennsylvania, forming the right wing; those of Maryland and Virginia would come together at Fort Cumberland, Maryland, and form the left. The two columns were to merge at Bedford, Pennsylvania, on September 10.

Washington agreed, though without enthusiasm. He had little faith in the militia system, which had worked so badly for him in the Revolution.

The Secretary of War, Henry Knox, was consulted, though not much. He had been given a large grant of land in Maine by the government of his native Massachusetts (Maine was a part of Massachusetts) as a thank-you for his war services, and he was eager to get there and survey it and perhaps sell it. His plans had all been laid, but he offered to discard them and go through Pennsylvania with the Commander-in-Chief if this was thought necessary.

Hamilton said that it wasn't. Hamilton was familiar with the workings of the War Department anyway, for it was the practice of Congress to turn over in a lump to the Treasury Department all sums appropriated for the War Department, and the Treasury would then stipulate how this sum was to be divided. In addition, Hamilton had a strong personal hold over General Knox, one of his most ardent admirers. Therefore, let Knox go to Maine. The President could appoint Secretary Hamilton an Assistant Secretary of War to act in his place.

Washington agreed to do this. When, amid the cheers, the President left Philadelphia to lead the tossed-together army, he rode in an open carriage, his personal secretary Bartholomew Dandridge on his left side, and the Secretary of the Treasury, who was also Acting Secretary of War, on his right.

The first night out, at an inn, a courier arrived from wilderness headquarters. The army out there had been badly mauled on two recent occasions, under Generals Harmar and St. Clair, but now, under Wayne, it had won a resounding victory at a place called Fallen Timbers. It had followed this success by scattering the Indians throughout the Northwest Territory, burning their villages, and uprooting their fields. This did not mean that the United States Army was now available east of the mountains, or that it could be counted upon to help put down the revolt of those red-eyed yahoos of Appalachia, but it did lift a worry off General Washington's mind, enabling him to make the rest of the trip in a receptive spirit.

That trip was not a triumphal march, but it did do a great deal for the Commander-in-Chief, whose popularity with the troops seemed as great as ever. He was huzzahed everywhere. He was, as in earlier days, "loved as a father, as a god adored," which was a great comfort to him, a relief as well.

The militiamen as a whole acted in a most exemplary manner. Virginia, like Pennsylvania, had found some difficulty in filling its quota, and all who went were not, really, volunteers; but in the circumstances they behaved admirably. They stole very little, and did not even rouse much hard feeling in the villages and towns through which they passed, towns and villages filled with people who traditionally hated standing armies. Two civilians were killed, each because of a hastily handled military weapon, but these were accidents.

With four governors in the party, each the head of his own army, not to mention the Acting Secretary of War, there was some confusion about the chain of command on several occasions, and about individual jurisdiction, but this was not serious. Governor Mifflin of Pennsylvania got especially drunk one night and ordered an elite guard to fire upon any skulkers who looked as if they might be deserting, an order that could have caused a great deal of trouble if it had been obeyed. Fortunately it wasn't obeyed; and the governor apologized publicly the next morning.

To be sure, from the beginning the enterprise did suggest the use of a sledgehammer to swat a fly. The Whiskey Boys, as soon as they heard that the government meant business and was approaching in force, seemed to evaporate. The few who might have been made to face serious charges disappeared down the Ohio, never to be heard from again. The rest simply went home and remained there, denying everything. But the army, as is the way with military machines, could not be halted or turned back once it was in motion. Everything went according to schedule. A few prisoners were taken, and a few of these were mistreated, but not many, and not much. Even though it knew as soon as it had started that it would meet nothing, the army proceeded on its way as laid out. Washington did not go the whole distance to the Golden Triangle but turned back at Bedford, for he wished to be in Philadelphia in time for the opening of the new Congress on November 3. He left the senior ranking officer, Governor Henry Lee of Virginia, in charge.

Twenty prisoners actually were charged with treason and taken to Philadelphia, where they were marched through the streets for several hours, each with a sign on his hat reading "Insurrectionist." Then they were tried. Eighteen were acquitted. Two were convicted and sentenced to death. One of these was a halfwit, the other was practically that. President Washington pardoned them both.

The whole business had cost the government almost $1.5 million, much more than Mr. Secretary Hamilton had estimated.

Politically, legally, nothing had been resolved, nothing settled. But now everybody knew who the boss was.

Washington opened the new session of Congress with a speech —written for him by Edmund Randolph—that was notable chiefly for its excoriation of the Democratic Clubs, which he roundly declared to have been responsible for the whole thing. "These self-created societies," he stated, had promoted "the most diabolical attempt to destroy the best fabric of human government and happiness, that has ever been presented for the acceptance of mankind."

The Senate of the United States dutifully proposed to pronounce the clubs illegal, a decision in which the House, after five days of hot debate, refused to concur.

Whether or not it was because of the President's censure, the Democratic Clubs did very largely die out of their own accord after five or six years.

Alexander Hamilton, having made his point, resigned. He moved to New York City, and there, with a partner named Balthazar De Heart, he opened a law office in Wall Street, a small but fashionable uptown thoroughfare.

★ 10 ★

A Peephole for Lord Grenville

★ The Jay family, back in La Rochelle, France, had been rated —and thought of themselves—as middle class. After the revocation of the Edict of Nantes, they moved to England, for they were Huguenots, and they continued to be considered middle class. However, in America, a little later, they joined the aristocracy. They were traders and had always been prosperous. New Yorkers, they married with the Bayards, Stuyvesants, Van Cortlandts, and Phillipses; John Jay's own wife was a Livingston.

Certainly his nose was uptilted. A graduate of King's College (Columbia), he had quit the family world of commerce for law, at which he was highly successful, his clientele being, where his heart always was, among the rich. He was a Hamiltonian before he had even heard of Alexander Hamilton. Untouched himself by the mucilaginous fingers of greed, he believed that every man who could be considered quality should be permitted and even encouraged to make money. To him, gain was God, and he believed that those who owned the country ought to govern it. In 1790 he had, single-handedly, framed the constitution of New York State, the narrowest in the nation in matters relating to the property qualification of voters: of the 13,330 white male

New York residents of voting age at that time, only 1,303 could vote.

Jay looked the part. He was skinny, a rickle of sticks, and his dark disapproving eyes glared out from under brows that seemed to be made of wire. He might have held lemon juice in his mouth instead of spit. He could be friendly and even jovial, when he thought that he was in the presence of his equals, but there were not many of those.

This aloofness, this inner conviction that he was one of the favored few, should have won him a welcome among the English, who traditionally treat such an attitude with respect. Certainly Jay's position was high enough to dazzle them, and the record of his experience as a diplomat must have impressed the most blasé. He was not being hurried. He knew that he had his government behind him, for things in Philadelphia were firmly in the hands of men who thought as he did. His credentials were in order; his cause was just.

Why then did he come up with the worst treaty in the history of the United States?

The Treaty of Amity, Commerce and Navigation was no throw-together, no stopgap hastily designed for an emergency. It had taken many months to frame. Yet it granted almost nothing of what the States had hoped to get. Instead, it iterated Britain's own most outrageous demands, and its tone, unmistakably English, was that of a victor who condescends, not very graciously, to name terms to one who cringes in defeat.

Article 2 did decree a withdrawal of the military forces in the six wilderness forts, a *sine qua non* in Jay's instructions, but this was not to be done immediately, and there was no mention of indemnification.

Article 3 gave the British access to the headwaters of the Mississippi, which had not yet been discovered but were thought to be much farther east than in fact they are. That gave them a chance to get at the Spaniards in New Orleans in force without being obliged to ask for permission to march through United

States territory, because it specifically gave them full rights to the river. The same article also permitted American trappers or traders to go north of the Great Lakes region—in case, supposedly, any of them wanted to visit the frozen wastes of Hudson Bay.

Article 12 did permit a certain amount of American trade with the British West Indies, but this trade was to be subject to all sorts of onerous restrictions, and was not even to start until the war with France was over. The trade was to last but two years and was, moreover, to be confined to small vessels—70 tons or less. "A canoe fleet," James Madison hooted, when he heard of it.

There was no mention of payment for the Negro slaves stolen in the Revolution, nor any of reparations for American ships and cargoes seized on the high seas. The matter of trading debts should be left to a joint commission that would consist of four English members and three Americans.

There was no mention of impressment.

There was no mention of the American demand for the doctrine of neutral ships making neutral goods.

Why then did John Jay sign it?

There might be many reasons that we will never know, but there are a few that we do know.

Undoubtedly it had been impressed upon Jay, as he was preparing to depart, that above all, and regardless of the letter of his written instructions, he *must* get a treaty. Unless there was a treaty, and right away, there would be war. So they told him, and so, no doubt, he believed. War with Great Britain would be fatal to the weak, tottering United States of America; whereas Britain, on the other hand, as she showed in her high-handed behavior, her arrogance, not only meant to do nothing to avert such a war but might well be prepared to welcome it as an excuse to seize *all* American vessels on the high seas, regardless of cargo or the nationality of the crew.

Here was a mistake, but John Jay had no reason to think it a mistake. In fact, while Britain certainly did not fear war with the United States, that puny republic, she would have done a great deal to stave it off. The new nation, after all, was Britain's best customer, and the smattering of shipping that could be swept off the ocean in the event of war—for all American vessels assuredly would take to cover then, and stay there—was as nothing compared to the loss of honestly bought grain and, still more important, naval stores that war would entail.

Agriculture had reached a high stage of development in Great Britain, a nation that could almost feed itself, but this was not true in the matter of timber. More than ever, and more and more every year, Great Britain was to be dependent upon her navy. While she desperately needed men to handle the warships —and it didn't matter how she got them—she even more desperately needed masts, spars, planking, booms—but especially masts, the *big* timber. A few hundred years before, England had been almost all trees, but now it was almost all fields. No longer could the King's commissioners roam the forests of Gloucestershire and Hampshire, also those of the American colonies, marking the tallest pines and oaks for the future use of the Navy. There were no longer any tall trees—there were very few trees at all— in Hampshire and Gloucester, and the American colonies had become independent.

There was also the prosaic but highly important matter of that product of pine: pitch. The Royal Navy, for the first time in history, was trying to clamp a blockade upon a whole nation, France, and this called for an unending stream of tar. Most of it came from the Baltic states and from the Carolinas and Georgia. There were dark rumors that the nations of the late Armed Neutrality League—Denmark, Sweden, Prussia, Russia—might get together again in an attempt to offset the British Navy. Sweden, which then included Norway, was one of the two main sources of pine products for Great Britain. If it *and* the other main source, the United States, should be cut off by war, what would happen to that grand blockade of France? And what, indeed, would happen to the "sceptered isle" itself?

The British, then, would have done a great deal to avoid a

rupture with the United States, but being British, and being skilled diplomats as well, they concealed this, and John Jay, like the men who had sent him, seems never to have suspected it.

He was, habitually, a disapprover. He was holier than thou, and by far. He was the very epitome of austerity. Yet there was a chink in his icy armor. As soon as he was appointed to the post, and long before he stepped ashore in England, the word went out at Whitehall—the British, then as now, had the best intelligence service in the world—that "Mr. Jay's weakness is Mr. Jay." They all but fawned upon him, as they whittled down his demands. He had dinner with Mr. Pitt, with Lord Grenville, also with the Lord Chancellor. He was presented to the King, who praised him. He liked this.

After a while, though, pleasant as the talks with Lord Grenville were, Jay waxed uneasy. He sensed that his confrere was marking time, looking for something, perhaps waiting for something, though infallibly polite. He was right. William Wyndham Lord Grenville, the Foreign Minister, had used well the spy services at his command. He knew that Jay, despite his instructions, personally believed that the British were justified in keeping the six wilderness forts, in view of the unpaid American debts, and he knew too that Jay, an abolitionist, though he saw that refusal to pay indemnity for the Negro slaves taken in the Revolution was *technically* a violation of the Treaty of 1783, believed that it was *morally* defensible—and wouldn't press this demand too hard.

What Grenville did not know was whether or not Sweden and Denmark had asked the United States to join them in a renewed Armed Neutrality League, a naval organization that could play hob with Britain's blockade of France. If they had, what response would the new nation give, what stand would it take? There had been no reference to the Armed Neutrality in Jay's official instructions, but perhaps he was saving it for use as a surprise weapon. There was no mention of it in the ambassador's mail—and it must be assumed that British intelligence was opening John Jay's mail at this time, as was its custom. We do know from the recently published Grenville papers that "Whitehall" had been their private code name for Jay, though Jay did not know this.

Troubled, though outwardly affable as always, Lord Grenville wrote to the British ambassador at Philadelphia, suggesting that he ask Alexander Hamilton about the League.

Hamilton was no traitor! He was as patriotic as the next man. But he conceived the future of the new nation to be inextricably enmeshed with that of Great Britain, and he passionately wished for a commercial treaty between the two countries to fix this in place. When, even before the adoption of the Constitution, he met Lieutenant Colonel Edward Beckwith, an aide of Lord Dorchester, Governor General of Canada, he talked freely. Even after the Constitution had been adopted, even after Hamilton had become the first Secretary of the Treasury, he talked.

Beckwith was not in uniform, and he carried no credentials. He was visiting the States informally, his purpose being to learn how their leading politicians regarded the situation vis-à-vis Great Britain. He was an officer who had been trained in intelligence work, a good listener, himself close-mouthed, and he reported direct to Lord Dorchester in Canada. Dorchester of course forwarded those reports to the Foreign Office in London. All this was unofficial. Britain never committed herself.

There was nothing sinister about Beckwith, who made several visits to the former colonies. He was simply doing a job. General Schuyler, who had introduced him to his son-in-law Alexander Hamilton, he found useful, as was also that other Tory-minded statesman, Senator Samuel Johnson of Connecticut. Hamilton himself was a gold mine. He gave Beckwith all the information he sought about Cabinet meetings. Some of these conversations Hamilton reported to Washington, but none was reported to the Secretary of State, Thomas Jefferson.

When, eight years after Great Britain had recognized American independence, she decided that it was safe to send an official ambassador to the new nation, he of course took over Beckwith's duties in this regard. He was George Hammond, an extremely intelligent young man—in his lower thirties when he reached Philadelphia—who found among his instructions a hint that he get acquainted with the Secretary of the Treasury. This he did, promptly.

Hamilton continued to be most cooperative. They met almost every day. *Formally* Hammond conferred with Jefferson, just as *formally* he had presented his credentials to Washington, the President, but Alexander Hamilton was his confidant, his chum, whose words he passed along to Whitehall. This was why Lord Grenville had written to Hammond about the Armed Neutrality matter.

He got Hammond's answer on September 20. The ambassador had talked with Mr. Secretary Hamilton about the situation, and Mr. Hamilton had declared unequivocally that the United States, which had indeed been approached by the Scandinavian countries, would have no part in such a movement. It was true, Mr. Secretary Hamilton had told the ambassador early in July that the new Secretary of State, Edmund Randolph, like his predecessor, sought to balance France against Great Britain, taking advantage of their state of warfare, and would have liked to hold the threat of such an alliance in check for future use, but he had been voted down. The President himself was convinced that this would have been the wrong course. They had Mr. Secretary Hamilton's word for it.

That was all Lord Grenville needed. In Jay he faced an unarmed foe, a man who could not hit back. Expertly he turned the screw, and the result was the infamous Jay's Treaty.

New York State politics were the dirtiest in the land, and when Jay, in his absence, had been elected governor of that state, it was not because of his popularity—he scorned popularity, which indeed was never thrust upon him—but because the politicos felt ashamed of the way they had cheated him out of the gubernatorial post two years before. This meant that he must resign the Chief Justiceship, as he gloomily realized. He realized too that the voters wouldn't cheer him any longer once they heard of the treaty he had just negotiated. He had no illusions about that and confessed in letters to friends that he believed it was the best that could have been done in the circumstances. The American public was thus, in a small way, steeled against the shock.

When John Jay came to send the treaty to the States for ratification, it was as though the fates had conspired to delay the jolt that he knew to be inevitable. What with British cruisers and French privateers, no man's ship was safe in the North Atlantic, and Jay dispatched copies of the treaty, as was the custom, by three different vessels. The first was captured by French privateers; the second, badly battered by a storm, was forced to put back to an English port; and only the third, the slowest of them, got through.

The treaty was signed in London on November 19, 1794. It was the middle of March before President Washington, in Philadelphia, was handed a copy.

He read it, and turned pale. He sent for Randolph.

Randolph, the second Secretary of State, was no longer known as a weathervane. Despite his denunciation of the "self-created" Democratic Societies, in general he favored the liberal French line of his predecessor, Thomas Jefferson, and Hammond hated him. In the Cabinet Randolph's was, again and again, the minority report.

Of the other members, William Bradford, the Attorney General, was a Federalist, though a moderate one, but he was ill and close to death. Timothy Pickering in the War Department and Oliver Wolcott, Jr., Hamilton's successor in Treasury, were both New Englanders, both High Federalists, followers of Hamilton, and could be counted upon to swallow any English affront.

These others were not called in. Washington and Randolph, fellow Virginians, old friends, wrestled with the problem alone.

They decided, at last, not to decide anything. The President kept the horrid paper in his desk for several months before he called a special session of the Senate to consider it. He presented the thing without comment.

The Senate, thirty members, esteemed itself a very exalted body indeed, though it was in the House that the really hot debates were held, the really telling votes registered. It was in the House that James Madison deployed his parliamentary troops, and the opposition was strong. In the Senate, predictably, the Federalists had things their own way.

Senate sessions were always secret. This time, however, the Senators outdid even their own hushhushness by pledging all of their members *in advance* to give out no information about the treaty, the debate-to-be, or the result of the final vote. The Republican-Democrats objected, but they were outnumbered.

The Senate, always conservative and still a Federalist stronghold, was nevertheless not as one-sided as it had been a little earlier. Sundry Republican-Democrats had squirmed in, somehow, at a recent election, among them a soft-spoken, sweet-smiling little lawyer from New York who had had the temerity to defeat the captain of the Hamiltonian team in the upper house, General Schuyler, whose seat he now occupied. This villain, named Aaron Burr, led the fight against ratification of the Jay Treaty. Hamilton never forgave him.

Meanwhile, the world outside seethed with rumors about the pact with Great Britain, which was reported to call for little less than a military alliance. All sorts of stories swirled through the streets and the drawing rooms of Philadelphia. The new French ambassador, Jean Antoine Joseph Fauchet, who was almost as objectionable as Genêt had been, did everything he could to get a peek at the Jay report, but his efforts were in vain. France feared the worst and was prepared to denounce this mysterious treaty as a violation of the Franco-American treaty of 1778. The American ambassador in Paris, young James Monroe, had asked John Jay for a copy, but Jay, who abhorred him, coldly refused.

After what must have been some memorable wrangling, the Senate at last ratified the treaty and sent it back to the President for signature. The Constitution calls for a two-thirds vote in such cases, and it was that exactly, and no more, in the Senate— 20 to 10.

Washington still worried about the thing, and he kept it in his desk for more than a month, not signing it until August 14.

Meanwhile, a Republican Senator, Stevens Thomson Mason of Virginia, after disclaiming his oath of silence, had handed a copy of the treaty to the most malific Republican editor of them all, Benjamin Franklin Bache ("Lightning Rod Junior"), a grandson of the Good Doctor, who hailed it as "an imp of darkness, illegitimately begotten," and had it printed as a pamphlet.

It might be supposed that after all the secrecy and after all the wild reports the public would greet the text of the treaty, bad as it was, with downright relief. This was not so. The public set up a howl that was loud and long. Resolutions by the score were passed, denouncing the thing as a sellout, begging the President to refuse to ratify it. This was done not just by the still operating Democratic Societies but by open mass meetings attended by Republicans and Federalists alike. Some of the most respected Federalists, indeed, John Dickinson, Charles Pinckney, John Langdon, quit the party in disgust. Copies of the treaty were burned in front of the British embassy and the British consulates in Boston, Charleston, Philadelphia, and New York. Stones were thrown at speakers who started to defend it, though these were few. John Jay was hanged in effigy, in the North and South but especially in the West, where he had always been hated as an effete snob. He paid no attention. He simply said, once more, that he had done what he'd been sent out to do—he had averted war with Great Britain.

But what about war with France?

★ 11 ★

First in the Hearts

★ George Washington was frightened. He was the man who had braved the wilderness when it really was wild, whose coolness under fire again and again had starched his troops, the man who even seemed to *enjoy* danger—"I heard the bullets whistle, and, believe me, there is something charming in the sound," he had written to his brother John after his first brush with the foe in the French and Indian War—so it must not be supposed that it was *physical* fear that afflicted him. He had trained himself well, and he would not have known how to quake. No, he wasn't afraid for his life: he was afraid for his country.

The worst that could have happened had happened, the thing he had dreaded most. The country was split into two parties. Back in the days of the first Cabinet, the differences between Mr. Jefferson and Mr. Hamilton, though admittedly they were concerned with the very makeup of the state, had seemed like no more than a family spat that would soon pass away and be forgotten. Now it was more like open war, and General Washington, who was tired, did not want war.

The Anglomen were calling the Gallomen Jacobins, the Gallomen were calling the Anglomen monocrats, and all the voices scraped with hatred. *Everything* was political these days. Moreover, the matter was getting worse. In the Second Congress, when Mr. Hamilton had fairly pelted the legislative branch with his intricate and beautifully worked-out plans for remaking the nation, the President had been told that party cohesion was 58 percent. Today, in the so-called Jay Treaty Session, the first session of the Fourth Congress, it was 93 percent, and the few who did try to refrain from a regular taking of sides were sneered at as "whimsical, kinkish, and unaccommodating."

Like Londoners, men in the United States now patronized only public houses that were patronized by others of their political persuasion. Men crossed the street in order to avoid meeting political foes, even though they might be their relatives or onetime associates. Men refused to shake hands. Senator Charles Pinckney, a former governor of South Carolina, and Charles Cotesworth Pinckney were second cousins, but C.C., a Federalist, would not even speak to the Republican-Democrat Charles. In the small town of Dedham, Massachusetts, there were two brothers who resolutely scorned to recognize one another's existence: Fisher Ames, a sophistical rhetorician inebriated by the exuberance of his own verbosity, a member of the House of Representatives, and a Hamiltonian of the first water, and Dr. Nathaniel Ames, who characterized the Federalist party as "the Prigarchy."

At one time the Republicans had been brushed aside as cranks and crackpots, men who were blindly opposed to the national Constitution, though they were led by James Madison, the "Father" of that instrument, and also by Thomas Jefferson, propounder of strict constructionalism. That day had passed. Some High Federalists still referred to the Republicans as "anti-government men," as though they were so many anarchists, but the new party continued, quietly and mysteriously, to grow.

In the Fourth Congress, which assembled for its first session in December of 1795, these "anti-government men" for the first time constituted a recognizable majority. The Senate remained in the hands of the Federalists, to be sure, but the much more important House of Representatives now numbered fifty-seven Republican-Democrats, forty Federalists, seven independents.

In the days of the war Washington had been wont to call his

staff his "family." The aides were mostly young men, bright men, who adored him. He ate with them, drank with them, traveled with them, and he knew that he could depend upon them to give him an honest answer every time he asked a question. Now, with his advisory council, or Cabinet—his "heads of Departments and the Attorney General"—it was different. His was, as before, the sole responsibility, but his advisers couldn't seem to agree on anything.

The gamecocks were gone. Mr. Jefferson rusticated at Monticello, where it was said that he was much more interested in potatoes than in politics, and Mr. Hamilton was in New York, where he made money practicing law and lost it again in his ill-starred Society of Useful Manufactures (S.U.M.) and in land speculation. Yet the differences between these two seethed on, if not within the President's hearing.

Mr. Jefferson would make no public statement and take no public stand, but he was known to be knitting the Gallomen together by means of his personal letters to friends, and even in retirement he was considered the head of an increasingly large opposition party. He had called the Jay treaty "that execrable thing" and "this infamous act," and his assertion that "acquiescence under insult" was no way to escape war was much quoted.

As for Mr. Hamilton, for all the press of his work in the New York courts, he was always ready when asked—and sometimes even when he had not been asked—to give a long, acute analysis of any problem the Chief Executive might meet, together with a final answer, a definitive solution. Colonel Hamilton had been one of "the family," and the President was accustomed to his advice. But—perhaps he was *too* accustomed to this? Men said so, he had heard. Men said too that Colonel Hamilton took advantage of this report, took advantage of his reputation as a power behind the throne.

The President didn't like to think that such rumors were going the rounds. Then, too, there was the matter of the mails. New York was a long way from Philadelphia, and even the fastest riders took better than two days, a time that could be greatly and inexplicably lengthened. The President had heard, for example, that when the insufferable Citizen Genêt had been in New York in the early fall of '93, to help quell a mutiny in the French fleet fresh up from Martinique, he had mailed a letter on September 18 to Thomas Jefferson in Philadelphia, which letter got to the Secretary of State on December 2.

The President himself had always been conscientious about his letter writing, answering everything promptly and fully, whether he penned the reply in person or through a secretary. The avalanche of mail that had descended upon him after the publication of the Jay treaty, however, had caused him to drop this lifelong habit. The letters came from all fifteen of the states, and those that were from official bodies, like the Virginia House of Assembly, were the only ones he officially answered. Others, however, those that seemed to him irresponsible or insolent, many of them from the very "self-created societies" he had condemned, he read and shoved aside. The bundle of these was growing bigger every day, a reproach. Was this part of getting old?

When Edmund Randolph resigned—in a splutter of recriminations, to write and publish his confused and splenetic *Vindication,* in which he accused the President of being a tool of the British party and a faithless friend to boot—it might have seemed to Washington for a little while that peace would come to the Cabinet, where the Secretary of State had been the only Southerner, the only Republican as well. But this was not to be. Not only was Washington troubled by the hard feelings the resignation had caused, not only did he miss Randolph, an old friend, the only Virginia gentleman left in the political "family," the only adviser with whom he could speak familiarly, but he learned as well, to his dismay, that the Secretary would be hard to replace. Did this mean that good men were reluctant to serve under him, George Washington? Did it mean that they doubted the durability of the government?

The President had first offered the post to Supreme Court Justice William Paterson of New Jersey (Paterson, New Jersey, was named after him), but the man who had led the small-state faction in the Constitutional Convention of 1787, an S.U.M. associate of Colonel Hamilton, refused. Then Governor Thomas Johnson of Maryland also refused to become the nation's third Secretary of State, as did Charles Cotesworth Pinckney and Patrick Henry.

The Patrick Henry nomination might seem a strange one for George Washington to have made, but "the forest-born Demosthenes," the give-me-liberty-or-give-me-death man, the southern opposite number to Samuel Adams of Massachusetts, no longer was the loudest radical of them all. As his arteries hardened, as his pulse slowed, Patrick Henry became more and more conservative. He no longer thundered. A successful courtroom lawyer, a man of much property now, he would sit tight, tut-tutting all proposals for change.

The President then tried Rufus King, a New Yorker, a High Federalist, and John Marshall, a fellow Virginian, but both of them also declined.

All this while, too, the President was seeking, almost beseechingly, successors to the Attorney General, William Bradford, who had died, and Chief Justice Jay, who had resigned. Nobody seemed to want those important posts either. Why?

He at last persuaded a Massachusetts man, the sour-visaged Timothy Pickering, who had been Postmaster General (not a Cabinet post then) to accept State. Oliver Wolcott, Jr., of Connecticut—President Washington had never liked New Englanders, though he scrupulously concealed this distaste—became Secretary of the Treasury, a faithful follower in Hamilton's footsteps, though he had none of Hamilton's managerial ability. James McHenry of Maryland, an amiable man but scarcely an enlightened adviser, became Secretary of War. Charles Lee, another nonentity—but at least he hailed from Virginia—became Attorney General.

Washington was not pleased with the result of this reshuffle, but he believed that he had done the best he could. He was tired.

It might be supposed that after the President signed the Jay treaty and made it the law of the land, the howl of the protesters would subside. It was not so. Mass meetings continued to be held, resolutions of resentment kept pouring in. The West had been mollified, at least in part, by the wonderful treaty brought back from Madrid by Thomas Pinckney, the special envoy Washington had recently appointed for that purpose. The Mississippi was open, and that was good, but otherwise the situation seemed little changed.

Fisher Ames, who had entered Harvard at the age of twelve and never got over it, roundly declared that "the treaty will go in spite of mobs," and Alexander Hamilton, when asked, advanced the belief that "the treaty is in no way inconsistent with national honour" and that "the great and cardinal *sin* of the treaty in the eyes of its adversaries is, that it puts an end to controversy with Great Britain."

However, the British navy went on enforcing the obnoxious orders in council, impressing American seamen from American ships on the high seas, and seizing American cargoes. What Ambassador James Monroe had predicted was coming about: France, furious, was regarding the Jay treaty as a breach of her own 1778 treaties with the American republic, as virtually a military alliance with Great Britain, indeed as an act of war. She too began seizing American ships.

To make matters even worse, in the spring of that year 1796, the last full year of Washington's administration, the House of Representatives erupted.

The Constitution provides that treaties shall be made by the President with the advice and consent of the Senate. The House is not even mentioned in this connection. The House had been quiet of late. It had a slim Republican majority, but the Republican leader, little James Madison, had been absent, taking a rest in the Virginia hills with his bride, the full-blown Dolley. Madison was back now, but it was another Congressman, Edward Livingston of New York, who exploded the bomb. Early in March he offered a motion that would have called upon the President to hand over to the House the full text of Jay's instructions before he went to London, together with all of his official correspondence and everything else connected with the case, "except such papers as any existing negotiations may render improper to be disclosed."

Here was another *new* thing, another first case. Once again the President would be called upon to set a precedent.

Admittedly the House was not given Constitutional control of the making of treaties, Livingston went on, but the House was given control of appropriations, all of which must originate there. The House was about to be called upon to vote money for the enforcement of Jay's treaty, and therefore the House was entitled to know, in detail, the circumstances that had brought this treaty into existence.

Though it horrified Hamilton, here was the doctrine of implied powers all over again, and with a vengeance.

Washington stood firm. There were many things he did not know about fine points of law, but he knew a fight when he saw one. He said no.

The debate lasted five days and was one of the most memorable ever to be held in the House. The Vice President and the Senate attended every day in a body, and so did everybody else who could get in. Though the Republican-Democrats had control of the body and though in general their parliamentary discipline was better than that of the Federalists, the Livingston motion eventually was lost—by a vote of 51 to 48. The enforcement funds were appropriated.

The Federalists and the President—it was no longer possible to consider them apart from one another, despite Washington's dogged insistence that he must be above party—had won. But the chasm was deeper than ever and wider.

The President turned with a sigh to his desk. It was time, he reckoned, to rewrite his Farewell Address.

★ 12 ★

A Word to Posterity

★ He had conceived this project four years ago, when he was preparing to close up Presidential affairs and return to Mount Vernon. He knew that he was a poor speaker, subject to stage fright that made him mumble, and he had planned to cast his good-bye thoughts into the form of a written "address." He had made notes, then gathered them and arranged them into an outline. He knew what he wanted to say, but he wasn't sure how to say it. He had turned over the whole business to one of his most trusted aides of the moment, James Madison.

Madison, like Hamilton, like Jefferson, was a poor speaker —oratory was not important in American politics at that time— but he was an excellent penman. He had reduced the President's jumble of ideas to long, firm-flowing sentences; he made it literary. The President was delighted. They had talked it over, changing a word or a phrase here and there until they had it just where George Washington wanted it. Then it had been filed away for future use.

That had been back in '92, when his first term of office was about to run out and he was making it clear to his associates that he would not stand for another. Then on all sides they were expostulating with him, and they pointed out, the veins of their faces pulsating, that without his guidance the country would disintegrate. They meant it, and in time he came to agree. He had consented to stand for a second term. Now he wished that he hadn't.

His governmental troubles until that time had been domestic, but with his second term they became increasingly foreign—and menacing. War loomed, whether here or there. The French went mad, killing their monarchs, passing through a succession of fiery forms of rule, like so many flaming hoops—Girondists to Jacobins to Committee of Public Safety to Directory—while their massive armies marched back and forth across Europe, shouting slogans. The English, for their part, had suddenly ceased to regard their strayed American children with leniency and began to ride rough-shod over all overseas rights. "Take sides!" everyone cried. But that was exactly what George Washington had wished *not* to do.

The newspapers too had begun to emit unseemly yawps, as though they had taken the beginning of his second term as a signal. Suddenly they were calling the demigod all sorts of names. He had always been sensitive to any form of criticism, and this hurt. The only remedy seemed to be retirement. "I do not intend to be longer buffeted in the public prints by a set of infamous scribblers," he wrote to John Jay. He longed to get back to the farm.

He took the valedictory out of his desk. He reread it. The thing had been planned to review only four years of administration, but there had been four different years since that time, and much more had to be said.

He could not send it back to Mr. Madison, suggesting an addendum. Mr. Madison—it was painful to the President to reflect that he thought of it this way—had gone over to the enemy. He was a leader of the Republican-Democrats, *the* leader in the arena.

The President sent it to Mr. Hamilton instead.

Hamilton pondered the paper, doctored it somewhat, and wrote besides a completely new version, always sticking to the points the President had made. He sent both drafts to Philadelphia.

This went on for some time, for the President was fussy and anxious to have everything just right. Not much of Mr. Madison's text remained when they were finished.

The process was interrupted by the need to appoint a new ambassador to France. James Monroe, a headstrong young man, a Virginia lawyer, was presently serving in that capacity. He had been appointed while the President was still striving to keep a geographic balance in the diplomatic corps. Monroe had been chosen to offset the impression made by his predecessor, Gouverneur Morris, a charming, wooden-legged aristocrat from New York who had offended the revolutionists by his active support of the then still living royal family. That had been in 1793, when the United States was demanding the recall of Citizen Genêt, and in the circumstances, when France requested the recall of Morris, the government in Philadelphia could hardly refuse. Morris, as much of a misfit as Genêt, though a more intelligent man, was summoned back and the ambitious young Monroe sent over in his place.

The trouble with Monroe was that he had been *too* enthusiastic about the French revolutionaries. He had carried it to the point of bad taste. He had waved the tricolor, cheered the king killers, and openly visited Thomas Paine, who was then languishing in a French prison and likely to lose his head at any time. He had shouted *Liberté, Égalité, Fraternité*. In other words, he had done what he was told to do. However, things had changed at home since the telling. President Washington had definitely gone over to the Federalists. The Jay treaty had been signed, and the Gallomen were in disrepute.

Thomas Paine, a smudged patriot recently released from jail, had published an open letter that excoriated President Washington—"treacherous in private friendship . . . a hypocrite in public life"—and Washington thought, mistakenly, that Monroe could have prevented it. Monroe's friends, Thomas Jefferson and Edmund Randolph, had left the government, and now Monroe's superior, the man to whom he must report and from whom he must take orders, was a vinegarish Yankee, Timothy Pickering, who abhorred him. It was necessary, therefore, to inform the ambassador that his services were no longer required. Gleefully Pickering did so.

A harder task was that of picking a successor to Monroe, and here again the President was assailed by fears of a waning popularity. Didn't men trust him anymore? He considered John Marshall, who refused, and Patrick Henry, who did the same. He considered William Smith of South Carolina, but didn't ask him for fear of another refusal. At last he persuaded a different Southerner, Charles Cotesworth Pinckney, to take the job. Pinckney * by birth and temperament alike was an aristocrat, but he must be made to do.

Now it was possible to return to the correspondence with Mr. Hamilton, which the President gladly did. They went over everything very carefully, at long distance.

Hamilton always had been a good writer, but now he excelled himself. The Farewell Address outdoes in eloquence even the famed *Federalist* papers—polysyllabic, yes; bumptious, never. It is an acknowledged masterpiece and confirms the belief that Hamilton wrote better when he was expressing somebody else's ideas than when he was expressing his own, for though the words of the Farewell Address might have been largely his, the *thoughts* were those of the President. In later years, after his death, worshipful relatives were wont to assert that Alexander Hamilton had written the Address, but he himself, though surely no man to hide his light under a bushel, never made this claim. He didn't *write* it, he *assembled* it.†

* All of the Pinckneys came from South Carolina. Thomas was the one who negotiated the Mississippi-opening treaty with Spain, and he ran on the ticket with John Adams in 1796, assumedly for Vice President. Charles Cotesworth was his brother, a Revolutionary War veteran, a former aide to General Washington. Charles ("Constitution Charlie") Pinckney, a cousin, was the only Republican in the family.

† The original is in the New York Public Library, which in 1935 published what must be called the definitive edition, a handsome book, complete with all versions, alterations, amendments, and a fine introduction by the editor, Victor Paltsits.

The Address starts with an assurance to the American people that the liberty they have won can always be theirs if they do not permit themselves to split into geographical or ideological factions. Not in the oleaginous voice of a politician, but rather with a deep, shining sincerity, the President assures them:

Respect for its [the government's] authority, compliance with its laws, acquiescence in its measures, are duties enjoyed by the fundamental maxims of true liberty. The basis of our political system is the right of the people to make and to alter their constitutions of government. But the constitution which at any time exists, till changed by an explicit and authentic act of the whole people, is sacredly obligatory upon all. The very idea of power and the right of the people to establish government presupposed the duty of every individual to obey the established government.

He inveighs against the overlapping or intermixing of government departments:

I have already intimated to you the danger of parties in the State, with particular reference to the founding of them on geographical discriminations. . . . It is important, likewise, that the habits of thinking in a free country should inspire caution in those intrusted with its administration to confine themselves within their respective constitutional spheres, avoiding in the exercise of the powers of one department to encroach upon another. The spirit of encroachment tends to consolidate the powers of all the departments in one, and thus to create, whatever the form of government, a real despotism.

On one point only did the addresser and his amanuensis differ, and there Hamilton prevailed. The President had long fondled the hope of having a national university—presumably named after him, though he never said so—established in the new capital-to-be, the Grand Columbian City on the Potomac. He would have incorporated this suggestion in the Address, putting it directly before the American people, but Hamilton persuaded him that it would be more fittingly contained in his annual message to Congress. The Address has only two lines devoted to education:

Promote, then, as an object of primary importance, institutions for the general diffusion of knowledge. In proportion as the structure of a government gives force to public opinion, it is essential that public opinion should be enlightened.

Religion was not omitted:

Whatever may be conceded to the influence of refined education on minds of peculiar structure, reason and experience both forbid us to expect that national morality can prevail in exclusion of religious principle.

Nor were the national bank and the money system it stood for forgotten:

Cherish public credit. One method of preserving it is to use it as sparingly as possible: avoiding occasions of expence by cultivating peace, but remembering also that timely disbursements to prepare for danger frequently prevent much greater disbursements to repel it.

It is not until the second half of the Address—actually, only about a third of the whole—that Washington got into the "entangling alliances" admonition. It should be noted that this very phrase "entangling alliances" occurs nowhere in any draft of the Address, early, middle, or final. Not Madison nor Hamilton nor Washington himself concocted it. Thomas Jefferson was the first to use it, "honest friendship with all nations—entangling alliances with none," in his inaugural address of March 4, 1801.

It has been called the Holy Writ of Isolationism.

Observe good faith and justice toward all nations. Cultivate peace and harmony with all. . . . A passionate attachment of one nation for another produces a variety of evils. . . . Against the insidious wiles of foreign influence (I conjure you to believe me, fellow citizens) the jealousy of a free people ought to be *constantly* awake, since history and experience prove that foreign influence is one of the most baneful foes of republican government. . . .

The great rule of conduct for us in regard to foreign nations is, in extending our commercial relations, to have with them as little *political* connection as possible. So far as we have already formed engagements let them be fulfilled with perfect good faith. Here let us stop.

Thus does he acknowledge the debt to France, and thus dismiss it.

In the end, he freely admits that in forty-five years of continuous service to his country, he must have made many mistakes, and he expresses the hope that God and his fellow Americans will forgive him for them.

He finished, solemnly:

Relying on its kindness in this as in other things, and actuated by that fervent love toward it which is so natural to a man who views it in the native soil of himself and his progenitors for several generations, I anticipate with pleasing expectation that retreat in which I promise myself to realize without alloy the sweet enjoyment of partaking in the midst of my fellow citizens the benign influence of good laws under a free government—the ever-favorite object of my heart, and the happy reward, as I trust, of our mutual cares, labors, and dangers.

It had been Washington's intention, all along, to have the Farewell Address published that summer, soon after Congress had adjourned, which would have given the voters plenty of time to think things over before the selection of electors, but Hamilton, in letters, talked him out of it. "I do not think," Hamilton wrote to the President on July 5, 1796, "it is in the power of the party to throw any slur upon the lateness of your declaration." He was lying. He knew that the later the Address was issued, the better for the Federalists, since the Republican-Democrats could not make any move toward picking a ticket unless and until they had been assured by President Washington himself that he would not run again. Hamilton kept inventing excuses to touch the paper up in this way or in that, though Washington was satisfied and said so.

It was not until Thursday, September 15, that the President summoned to the Deshler house David C. Claypoole, the editor of the *American Daily Advertiser,* a Philadelphia afternoon paper, and in the upstairs drawing room handed him a copy of the Address, which he said he hoped the journalist would find room for. It was not until Monday, the nineteenth, after Washington had carefully read and checked the proofs, that it was published. By that time the President was on his way back to Mount Vernon.

The *American Daily Advertiser* was of course a Federalist publication, and it printed the Address, in full, without comment. Soon other papers picked it up, and those that commented did so quietly, inoffensively. The thing indeed caused little stir. It was to take Americans a long time to appreciate and fully to misunderstand it. Not until a century and a quarter later, when it was needed as a club with which to belabor those who would have had the United States join the League of Nations, was it accepted as a classic.

★ 13 ★

A Malodorous Tale

★ Two members of the House of Representatives, Abraham Bedford Venable and Frederick Augustus Conrad Muhlenberg, in December of 1792 had approached James Monroe, then a Senator. They knew where some interesting information about Alexander Hamilton was to be had.

Muhlenberg and Venable were moderate Federalists who had grown alarmed at some of the Secretary of the Treasury's doings. They believed, and with good reason, that Hamilton was engaged in an operation designed to take over the federal government, and that his ability to do so lay in his personal power over President Washington. They never *said* as much—at least they never recorded the belief on paper—but they must have supposed that it was their duty as Americans to block this archfoe of democracy by any means within their command. The means now at hand was gossip.

It seems that one Jacob Clingman, an unsavory character who had once worked for Venable, had been thrown into jail on a charge of subornation of perjury in connection with a government fraud case. There were many such cases pending at that time, for it was when the Secretary of the Treasury was ushering in his monumental refunding plan. The country was in a financial dither, edging upon inflation. Speculators were pushing off into the wilderness with handfuls of cash they had borrowed from the banks at 2½ percent a month, in some cases as much as 1 percent a week, to return with government securities sold to them by backwoodsmen who had not heard of Mr. Hamilton's grand plan. The Secretary's own assistant, William Duer, had been involved in one such scheme and was in jail.

Venable had got Clingman out of jail, but had refused to do anything for Clingman's partner, one James Reynolds. Clingman, however, declared that Reynolds "knew something" and that he could "hang the Secretary of the Treasury."

Venable went with this interesting information to Muhlenberg, and the two together went to Senator Monroe, whom, in the absence from Philadelphia of James Madison, they might well have considered the parliamentary chief of the Republicans.

The three then visited James Reynolds in prison. He proved to be a poor witness, loud with threats, but he did tell the investigators that his wife had letters from Alexander Hamilton that would prove what he said, whatever that was.

They then called upon Mrs. Reynolds. She was a full-blown woman, habitually high-strung and not much more intelligible than her husband had been. Like him, too, she was given to mysterious mutterings anent justice. She seemed always to be about to faint, and she could turn on tears like water at a tap, but she did have many letters that were undoubtedly in the handwriting of the Secretary of the Treasury.

After that Monroe, Muhlenberg, and Venable debated whether they should go to the President with what they knew. Or, if not that, then what?

They were human. They decided to go to Hamilton himself first, and see if he could explain.

Hamilton was jolted, but he instantly agreed to make everything clear. They should come to his house at 79 South Third Street, Philadelphia, that night, he said, and he would lay the whole matter before them. Meanwhile he would seek a friend who could act as witness. He always liked to have everything witnessed.

They called upon Hamilton that night, and he let them in. The servants had been dismissed, and his wife Elizabeth was visiting her folks in Albany with the children. The comptroller of the treasury, Oliver Wolcott, was present.

When they were all seated, Hamilton told a sorry tale. Twice, embarrassed, Venable and Muhlenberg interrupted to say that it wasn't necessary to go on, but Hamilton cut them off. He insisted upon telling the whole story. Monroe did not speak.

It had started the previous summer—that is, the summer of 1791—when Maria Reynolds had come one night to his house. He had never seen her before and had never heard of her. She was weeping. Hamilton let her in.

She told him that her husband had left her and she was destitute. She wanted to get back to New York, where she had friends, and she had heard that he, Mr. Hamilton, himself a New Yorker, was always generous to those in distress. Would he lend her some money? He promptly acceded to this, but he had no cash on hand, he said. Could she come back tomorrow night, or, better, could he take the money to her house? She agreed and gave him her address.

Surely he knew what to expect when he went there the next night, nor did she leave him any doubt. He was ushered into her bedroom, and they both got undressed.

This went on for several months. They met two or three times a week, brief encounters but telling, sometimes in her house, more often in his, always at night. Mrs. Hamilton was away.

Then *Mr.* Reynolds appeared on the scene. He raved. He threatened all sorts of dire things, blustering on until Hamilton asked him point-blank how much he wanted. A thousand dollars, Reynolds said.

Hamilton, who was then engaged in preparing his historic *Report on Manufactures,* did not have a thousand dollars handy, but he soon made two payments: $600 on December 22 and $400 on January 3, 1792.

It shut Reynolds up, but only for a little while. Soon he was back, complaining that his home, like his heart, had been broken. His wife still loved Colonel Hamilton, he wrote. Why didn't the

Secretary take her again and keep her quiet? He, Reynolds, would stay away for the occasion. He also asked for a "loan." Hamilton "lent" him $135 in April, $350 in May, $50 in June, $200 in August. All this was according to his own accounts, for he kept track of everything, filing the receipts and the various notes from the Reynoldses, like the careful businessman that he was.

Hamilton now spread his hands before Monroe, Venable, Muhlenberg, and Wolcott. So there, he said, they were.

The visitors did not know what to say, and indeed their host gave them little chance to speak anyway. He pushed all the papers upon them—notes, letters, receipts, the whole business— and he called upon them to keep them in some safe place. He called upon them, at the same time, to pledge themselves to silence about everything he had said.

It is notable that Alexander Hamilton had been concerned entirely with his personal reputation as a government official. He was determined not to jeopardize the money machine he had built. The Treasury Department was his own child. If he fell, it fell, and this must not be allowed to happen. Nobody else could possibly manage the establishment of a national bank. Nobody else could ever convince the American people, as he had, that public debt is a public blessing.

Hamilton might have winced at what the world would think of his behavior. He might have weighed the private feelings of his wife, his children, and his in-laws. If he did, he said nothing of this to the visitors at 79 South Third Street. That the Secretary's reputation for professional integrity should suffer in any way from anything said by a brash underling like Reynolds would be unthinkable to anybody else. Yet it was from fear of this, and this alone, that Hamilton pledged the Congressmen to silence and gave them the papers.

It was agreed that Senator Monroe should keep these papers. He turned them over to the secretary of the House of Representatives, a personal friend, John Beckley. Beckley was an ardent Republican whom the Federalists were trying to get fired.

Soon afterward, Hamilton wrote to Monroe asking for copies of the papers. Monroe asked Beckley to make such copies, and Beckley did so, but he seems to have made another set of copies at the same time.

There the matter rested for several years. Hamilton, his system in full operation, resigned from Treasury and set up a law practice in New York, but he continued to be a power behind the throne even after John Adams became President. Hamilton had Secretary of State Pickering in his pocket, as the saying went, and it was he more than any other man who caused the recall of Ambassador James Monroe. Monroe knew this. They hated one another.

Then early in July 1797, in New York an extraordinary thing happened. A recent arrival from Scotland, James T. Callender, published *The History of the United States for the Year 1796* and a chapter of it contained the malodorous Reynolds-Hamilton story, complete.

Callender was a cantankerous little newshawk, who, even when he was sober, which wasn't often, stank. He had first offered his services to the Federalists, who turned him down, for they already had more dirty scribblers than they needed, and now Jefferson was backing him, at least in part.

Nobody would believe what such a man wrote, and Hamilton's friends advised him to ignore the book. He wouldn't. His personal honor was at stake, he cried. He wrote immediately to Muhlenberg, Venable, and Monroe—ignoring the fact that Monroe was on the high seas on his way back from France—and demanded an explanation. Venable and Muhlenberg wrote back that they had no idea how or by whom the information had been leaked.

James Monroe came raging back. He was ready to kill somebody, and almost immediately the opportunity to do so was offered to him. He had, in fact, barely unpacked.

Monroe was full of fire over his dismissal. Indignation flamed within him. He was a man with a mission. He meant to write a book. His treatment by Philadelphia had been a disgrace, a scandal. His untimely removal from office by this new man, Pickering, must be explained, in words that admitted of no doubt, to his fellow countrymen. He had always wanted to write a book anyway.

He did not mean to stay here in New York, only until he could get his land legs back and make arrangements for posting to Philadelphia, where he would demand an apology.

Before he could as much as grind his teeth, though, he was called upon by a servant who handed him a note from Alexander Hamilton. Colonel Hamilton, the note said, would do himself the honor to wait upon Mr. Monroe this afternoon at such-and-such time. Colonel Hamilton would be accompanied by a friend.

This was July 11, 1797.

Monroe knew what it meant, though he didn't yet know *why*. He summoned a friend of his own, Congressman David Gelston.

Hamilton wanted a fight. Hamilton always wanted a fight. He was involved most of the time in some near-fracas or other. While an aide of General Washington, he and another aide, John Laurens of South Carolina, had agreed to call out General Charles Lee, who they thought had spoken slightingly of their chief. They tossed a coin, and Hamilton lost, so that he was only acting as a second when Laurens winged the general. Hamilton had come close to a meeting in the field with Major Giles in 1781 and again with Commodore James Nicholson in 1795. He had threatened two Massachusetts men, William Dana and Colonel John Brooks, with challenges, but these men had backed out. There had been another near thing with Representative John F. Mercer of Maryland. When Hamilton had won the Widow Rutgers' suit for her, it had been an unpopular decision and a group of young New York hotheads conspired to challenge him one by one until they dropped him in his tracks.

This bravura plan had been whuffed out by their leader, Isaac Ledyard, and it is possible Hamilton never even heard of it, but it is significant that the conspirators did not doubt that the ex-Secretary would have accepted all their challenges.

When Hamilton had argued with an anti-Jay's treaty crowd a little while ago and had been hit in the face by a stone, he had shrugged and retreated, but when he heard that Maturin Livingston had commented on his "want of spirit" on that occasion, he promptly wrote to Livingston to demand an explanation, which he got.

Men like James Monroe simply took their gentility for granted, but Hamilton always seemed to feel that he must prove his. He now had a town house at 24 Cedar Street in New York, but it was no more than a *pied-à-terre*. His real seat was to be the mansion he was building far north of the city on seventeen acres of land (it still stands, a museum now, at 287 Convent Avenue), a truly ducal structure which, significantly, he had named The Grange. His mother he never mentioned and seldom said anything about his father, but he was always willing to let it be known that his grandfather had been Alexander Hamilton of Grange, Ayrshire, a direct descendant of the Hamilton of Cambuskeith. The family arms—*gules,* a lion rampant *argent,* betwixt three cinquefoils *ermine;* crest: an oak tree *proper;* motto: VIRIDIS ET FRUCTIFERA—could be found painted on the doors of his coach. These things, like the dueling code, were important.

Therefore, when Monroe saw that Hamilton's friend that afternoon was his brother-in-law John Barker Church, he knew for sure what was coming.

Hamilton told Monroe he wanted an explanation for the Callender story.

Monroe said that he wished to confer with Venable and Muhlenberg before he made his answer.

Hamilton said that everything Monroe said was false.

Monroe sprang to his feet. "If you say I represented you falsely, you are a scoundrel!"

Hamilton sprang to *his* feet. "I will meet you like a gentleman!" he cried.

"I am ready," cried Monroe. "Get your pistols!"

Gelston and Church were between them by this time, calling "Now, gentlemen, gentlemen!" The statesmen subsided, and Hamilton agreed to wait for Monroe's letter of explanation.

That letter, when it came, was not satisfactory. Monroe declared that he had put the papers into the care of a trusted friend in Virginia, though he did not name this friend.

Had he instructed Beckley to leak the papers? Probably we will never know. Beckley might have done it on his own, for the Federalists had just brought about his discharge.

At any rate there now ensued a considerable correspondence, five carefully framed letters on each side. Monroe stipulated that he must be allowed three months before any meeting took place, for he still meant to write that book justifying his mission to France. He went to Philadelphia, leaving a New York friend to look after his honor. Hamilton, for his part, named as his second Major William Jackson.

Monroe and Hamilton were like boys who shove one another, saying, "I ain't scared of you! I *dare* you to step over this line!" There was a difference, however. Not merely a scuffle in the dust and a bloody nose could result from this momentous misunderstanding, but death itself.

It was customary in these cases for the seconds to make every effort to prevent a meeting in the field. They were expected to be able to testify afterward that they had done everything possible to prevent a shooting. Usually their pleadings were mere show, the gestures that were expected of them. Monroe's representative, however, took his assignment seriously.

Monroe himself remained in Philadelphia, where he had demanded of the State Department desk space in which to write his defense, and he got it. He seemed to have assumed, like Hamilton, that a duel was inevitable.

Monroe's representative was a short, handsome man who seldom spoke, though he often smiled. It was said of him that he could charm the birds down out of the trees. His name was Aaron Burr.

It seemed to Burr, as he went over the papers—for everything was written down, of course, and in duplicate—that the reason it was so hard to reach an agreement to fight was because *each man thought that he had been challenged.* Yet neither would dare to back out. All the world knew of these negotiations, and to back out now, howsoever gracefully, would be to brand oneself a coward. These little boys must not be thought scaredy-cats.

Burr framed a statement of the whole dispute. It was meant to be a joint statement. It was a triumph of conciliatory argument. Monroe, in Philadelphia, studied it and approved it. He signed.

Hamilton took longer, but the thing in time came to make sense to him too, and *he* signed.

Nobody, it was agreed, would try to kill anybody else.

After that, James Reynolds drifted into oblivion, his charges with him.

Maria Reynolds divorced her husband, her lawyer in this proceeding being Aaron Burr, and married Clingman.

John Beckley was taken care of by Republican friends, who got him the job of librarian of the new Library of Congress.

Alexander Hamilton still believed that it was necessary for him to clear his honor, and against the tearful protests of his friends he wrote "Observations on Certain Documents contained in Nos. V. & VI. of 'The History of the United States for the Year 1796,' in which the Charge of Speculation against Alexander Hamilton, late Secretary of the Treasury, is fully refuted." This was published in Philadelphia in that same year of 1797, presumably at Hamilton's expense. It ran to more than thirty pages of text and more than fifty pages of appended documents, rehearsing the whole sordid affair, which it pronounced a political plot on the part of "the Jacobin Scandal-Club," for which, it declared, "the spirit of Jacobism" was responsible. Hamilton appears to have lost his head entirely when he penned this farrago of hollow plunks and firecracker poppings. A few students since that time have expressed the belief that he thought that by baring his shame he was somehow saving his country, but everybody at the time, friend and foe alike, agreed that it killed any chance the man might have had of becoming President of the United States. The Republican-Democratic party with whoops of delight picked up the thing, reprinting it as a pamphlet.

Thomas Jefferson, like Aaron Burr, smiled mysteriously but made no comment.

Callender, infuriated by Jefferson's refusal to give him another "loan," turned against his benefactor, whom he libeled virulently. Jefferson of course made no answer. Callender, penniless, facing debtors' prison, fell while drunk off a James River ferry face-down into shallow water and was drowned. Thus he died, people remarked, as he had lived—in mud.

James Monroe wrote a vindication of his diplomatic career that was quite as silly, though not as long, as Hamilton's "Observations." It was a resounding failure. Monroe blamed this on his publisher, who didn't advertise it enough, he said.

★ 14 ★

The Man in the Middle

★ Now a learned clown waddles onto the stage. The late George Jean Nathan once said that the two most pitiful persons he could think of were a defeated candidate for the Vice Presidency of the United States and a streetwalker unable to make a living at it. John Adams had not been defeated as a Vice Presidential candidate, but on the ticket with George Washington and afterward as the presiding officer of the United States Senate—without a vote— he had been just as dim.

It was not always thus. When the American people were first learning to lean on one another, when they first began to realize that independence might be real and not just a glittering star pinned high upon the wall out of reach, there had been no more doughty fighter than John Adams. From the beginning, though surely no warrior, he had been in the middle of the conflict, both fists swinging. His patriotism was more than just vocal. He had worked on committees of correspondence, he had worked in the various continental congresses, and when called upon to do so, he had worked as well in the courtroom, all in the cause of liberty and justice. He was the best-read man in America, but it counted for more that he was one of America's most successful lawyers. That he was steeped in history, theology, political science, and economics did not impress his countrymen, but that he won most of his cases did.

After he had passed through the gray fog of the Vice Presidency, it was different. Wisps of that fog clung to him, blurring his outlines, but undeniably, despite it, the fellow was ridiculous, not noble any longer, just silly.

John Adams was not only fat but quakingly, *obtrusively* fat. His Rotundity they liked to call him. He pouted. He strutted. He liked to roll resounding titles off his tongue, and to march, toddle rather, to a drumbeat no other man could hear.

Regard him, as the nation did, when he had emerged from the second office to stand up and be sworn in as President of the United States, an awesome moment. On one side was George Washington, the outgoing President, on the other Thomas Jefferson, the incoming Vice President, who had been sworn in a little earlier in the Senate chamber upstairs. These two men were both six-footers; they were erect, rigid with dignity. Jefferson, the slouch gone, wore a long blue frockcoat, single-breasted, buttoned to the waist, and his hair was lightly powdered and tied in a queue with a black silk ribbon. Washington was magnificent in black, and his hair was well powdered. There was a sword at his side, and it looked as if it belonged there, as if it were a part of the man. Jefferson did not carry a sword, for that would have been against his political principles.

The lumpy little man between these giants was clad in light drab cloth, an unobtrusive outfit, and he *did* wear a sword. The weapon looked too long for him, and the amused spectators were sure that if he tried to walk it would get between his legs and cause him to trip. He too affected an air of stern responsibility, but on him it looked like a defense. "What he thought his majestic appearance," remarked the Philadelphia *Aurora,* "was only sesquipedality of belly."

The grandfather of the man who wrote that, the late Benjamin Franklin, had been kinder. He had said of John Adams that "he is always honest, sometimes great, but often mad."

In truth, the poor man could not be certain of where he stood as he waited for the Chief Justice to administer the oath of office. *That* person hovered nearby, sharing the dais with Washington, Jefferson, and pudgy Mr. Adams. He too was tall, and in his black silk robes of office he looked even taller. He was Oliver Ellsworth of Connecticut, a High Federalist, who disapproved of Mr. Adams. He held a large black Bible as though it were a club.

It had been a close election. The throne had shaken.

The Constitution provided that electors should be named in each state according to the methods provided by those states, each state to get as many electors as it had Senators and Representatives in Congress. Some electors were elected by the people at large, and some—most—were appointed by the respective legislatures. There was no uniform rule.

Voting qualifications, too, were different in the different states. In a population of only slightly over 4 million at the time of the March 4, 1797, inauguration, women, slaves, Indians, and minors were not eligible to vote. Of the remaining citizens, the free, adult, white males, it had been estimated that almost five sixths were barred from the polls because they did not own enough property.

Each elector wrote two names on his ballot, the order in which he set them down meaning nothing. The man who got the largest number of votes in all became President, the man who got the second largest number became Vice President. No provision was made for parties, since the men who framed the Constitution by and large believed that they were creating a form of government that would never need a party organization.

This had worked all right the first two times, when Washington had been elected virtually by acclamation, and John Adams, certainly the new nation's most distinguished civilian, had easily led the rest in the field, becoming Vice President, a post in which he could gather no glory, though at least it put some check upon his talent for amassing enemies. Adams always had talked too much, aloud and on paper, but so long as he was Vice President nobody paid any attention.

The 1796 election had been different. It set a pattern.

The South, excepting South Carolina where there was believed to be much Federalist strength, would be solidly Republican, New England would be Federalist. The middle states were the ones that counted, and especially New York and Pennsylvania, the largest.

The issue—there was only one—was unchanged. The issue was: France or England? But personalities would be more important.

In the three years since Thomas Jefferson got out of the government he had been very busy at Monticello, building a nail factory, setting out 1,600 imported peach trees, trying to increase his production of wheat. Yet he had found time for the writing of many letters, and without ever having made a speech or issued any kind of public statement, he had greatly tightened and strengthened the party of which he was the unacknowledged head. When at last George Washington announced that he would step down, nobody who called himself a Republican-Democrat had the slightest doubt as to who would be that party's candidate.

The only question was about who would share the ticket with Jefferson as Vice Presidential candidate. Since Jefferson came from the South, the other man must come from the North. This stood to reason; it was axiomatic in American politics from the very first. No New England candidate could hope to cut into that territory's solid Federalist majority. New Jersey, Delaware, and Maryland did not have a large electoral vote, so it was between New York and Pennsylvania. Aaron Burr of New York was at last selected.

The Federalists were not so clear in their minds. John Adams, very strong in his native New England, would be the Federalist choice for President, that much was certain. But there were various possibilities, favorite sons, for the Vice Presidency, Thomas Pinckney being the one most often mentioned. The Federal party, in fact, was already beginning to split down the middle, the moderates resenting the high-handed methods of the Hamiltonians. Hamilton himself hated John Adams, who once had referred to him as "the bastard brat of a Scotch pedlar." Even more important, Adams was not a man who could be manipulated.

In previous Presidential elections there had been no opposition press worth mentioning. Now there was a noisy one. The Republican editors, having lately learned that they could traduce Washington himself without fear of retaliation, ignored the various Federalist Vice Presidential candidates but leaped upon John Adams with malicious glee. They concentrated not upon his ideas of a paternalistic government, which they probably could not have understood anyway, but on his pomposity, his inordinate vanity, his love of ceremony and empty form.

Adams, in Articles of Confederation days, had served briefly as ambassador to Great Britain, and he had been impressed by the British system of titles and stations, the framework of rank. He believed that this made government more even, more convenient, and like a fool he had said so when he got home. The Republican press whooped with joy over this seeming weakness—"worse than Washington," "King John the First?"—and in pamphlet after throwaway pamphlet they quoted from Adams' earlier works to show him up as a royalty-smitten sycophant, a king worshiper. This was unfair, and it was not very effective anyway.

The Federalist journalists were not as undignified as that but just as dirty. They took their cue from their leader, who, when both men were in the Cabinet, had attacked Thomas Jefferson in the public prints for his record as wartime governor of Virginia. Near the end of his administration there, Jefferson had been paid a surprise visit by a detachment of dragoons under the dreaded Banastre ("Bloody Ban") Tarleton, who stormed in through the front door while the governor, tipped off barely in time, ducked out the back. This, to the boy-hero Hamilton, was cowardice. To be sure, Governor Jefferson had had no bodyguard and had been himself unarmed. What should he have done? Try to hold off the dragoons with his fists? Or simply stand there and let them bag the author of the Declaration of Independence?

Of course he ran. It was the best thing he could have done for his country, and in any event it had nothing to do with the man's ability to conduct foreign affairs as Secretary of State twelve or thirteen years later. "Scorpion" (one of Hamilton's noms de plume) nevertheless had made the best of it.

In the Presidential campaign of 1796 the cry of coward had been raised again, but to little effect. The war was long past by that time, and after all, the Federalist candidate, Adams, was no hero either.

A more telling charge was that of atheism. Jefferson, in fact, was a Deist, who believed that a man's religious beliefs were his own business, but the Federalists screamed just the same. "If you want a CHRISTIAN president, vote for the men who will elect John Adams," they cried in pamphlet form.

Jefferson himself made no answer to either charge.

Alexander Hamilton did not depend upon his subsidized newsmen. He too could write persuasive letters, and he wrote to many of his New England followers, urging them to instruct the electors they picked to throw away their first ballot choice and vote only for the second, Thomas Pinckney. This, he said, would help to offset the expected South Carolina movement to vote for Pinckney and Jefferson, two Southerners, rather than for Adams and Pinckney, and it would make for a fairer election. Nobody was fooled by this. It was patent even to his most devoted disciples that Hamilton, faced with what looked to him like a choice between two evils, was trying to euchre his own party's Presidential candidate out of the chief magistracy in favor of Pinckney, a man he knew well, a man he could manage.

The election was close and confusing. Not until late in December, after the electoral college had met, were the results known.

The New England Federalists had not obeyed their master. Three Massachusetts electors did throw away their second ballots, those for Pinckney, clearly in an attempt to save the Presidency for the regular party candidate, their own John Adams. The five Connecticut electors, all Federalists, gave their second ballots to John Jay instead of to Pinckney. The four Rhode Island electors gave theirs to a favorite son, and so did the six from New Hampshire. South Carolina did indeed support Jefferson, giving him and their own Thomas Pinckney all 8 of the state's electoral votes. Virginia gave 20 to Jefferson, 19 to Samuel Adams, and only 1 to Burr, though Jefferson had specifically promised Burr all twenty.

The final result was 71 for Adams, 68 for Jefferson, 59 for Pinckney, 30 for Burr, 28 scattered.

This meant that Adams had been elected President and Thomas Jefferson Vice President. His Rotundity was not even going to have a partner of his own persuasion. He would stand alone, the President by 3 votes.

So he waited, rehearsing in his mind the oration that he would soon be called upon to deliver, wishing that Abigail was out there among those long-faced statesmen to give him heart for the task ahead, and thinking, from time to time, of the applause that had greeted George Washington on his entrance into this chamber, the applause that had greeted Thomas Jefferson, and the lack of applause that had greeted *him*.

He was not even sure that he and Abigail could afford the Presidency. It paid $25,000 a year, to be sure, but he had already contracted to rent a house for $2,700 annually, while a carriage would cost at least $1,500, and horses at least $1,000 more—besides wine, besides silver and servants and swords for special occasions, all of these being expenses he had never faced before.

So he stood there. He prayed sometimes, a little, though without moving his lips and without closing his eyes. He hoped that, when it came time to walk off the platform, he could handle that sword at his side in such a way that it would not cause him to trip and fall.

Justice Ellsworth loomed, a mighty figure of a man in fluttering black. He held his right hand high, palm out, and extended the Book in his left.

"John Adams, do you solemnly swear . . ."

★ 15 ★

Messieurs X and Y and Z

★ It was John Adams who first experienced the American Presidential honeymoon. Indeed, he could be said to have introduced it. His was not a long one.

His inaugural appearance had been unfortunate, true, but his opening address to Congress was widely praised, even the Republican-Democrats finding good things to say about it. Uncertain of what was expected of him, or even of what was legal—since there was no mention of a Cabinet in the Constitution—Adams did not appoint advisers of his own but simply continued the ones Washington had left: Pickering in State, Wolcott in Treasury, McHenry in War, Charles Lee as Attorney General. This council was admittedly weak as compared with the original one, but it seemed to work well enough—at first.

The House of Representatives was back under Federalist control, where the Senate had always been. In the latter body, when a Republican member proposed a Constitutional Amendment to set up separate Presidential and Vice Presidential ballots in the electoral college, it was voted down, which seemed to endorse the system under which John Adams had been elected.

The Vice President, though nominally the leader of the opposition, seemed content to mumble through his duties as presiding officer of the Senate and did not lead any organized assault upon administration policies. Jefferson still believed that government should be "frugal and unassuming," that it should be "a few plain duties to be performed by a few servants," and Americans in increasing numbers seemed to agree. He had not sought the Vice Presidency; he never did remind Adams that Adams' victory had been by a mere 3 votes. Indeed, when Hamilton's divisive party tactics placed the electoral count in doubt for a little while, Jefferson in all seriousness proposed to Adams that in case of a tie he, Adams, take over the executive seat with the blessings of the man from Monticello.

Jefferson had been variously called "an intellectual voluptuary," "a howling atheist," and "a visionary philosopher," but he was working all the while—unobtrusively, as became a Vice President —for a better party organization, a clearer understanding among his followers, and sterner discipline. He had learned, as Madison promised, that in Philadelphia, in close daily touch with the lesser Republican leaders, he could accomplish much more than he had previously been able to accomplish by letters. None of this activity, of course, showed on the surface. Jefferson, as soon as he was sworn in, had called upon the new President and assured him of his willingness to help in any way.

Hamilton had done the same thing, but by letter, which letter had been long and dictatorial, covering just about everything, explaining everything to its addressee as though he had been in fact a backward child.

"I read it very deliberately," Adams said afterward, "and really thought the man was in a delirium."

Hamilton had meant well, but he had an unfortunate manner. Jefferson was not like that. Jefferson *believed* in his fellowmen, who, in consequence, began to believe in him.

France was the one cloud in the sky, and it was a dark cloud, dangerously low, scowling upon the land. C. C. Pinckney had been appointed to replace Monroe there as ambassador, as one of the last official acts of the retiring President, George Washington. But the French, all one snarl, bitter about the Jay treaty, which they considered neither more nor less than a commercial treaty with Great Britain in violation of the Franco-American treaties of 1778, had refused to accept his credentials. Moreover, the French Directory had framed that refusal in terms so insulting, so biting, that Pinckney, always the perfect gentleman, had retreated in confusion to Holland, whence he wrote home asking for advice.

This infuriated the American people, already irked by the interference in the election of 1796 of the French ambassador at Philadelphia, Pierre Adet, "that political blunderbuss," Fauchet's successor, who had campaigned for Jefferson.

All this while there were eighty American ships, together with their crews, interned at Bordeaux for some fancied offense, and now the Directory announced a complete blockade of the British Isles and began to seize American vessels right and left. More, the Directory decreed that any American sailor found serving on a British warship, *even if he could prove that he had been impressed,* would be hanged as a traitor.

A howl of rage arose from all sixteen states, a louder and more menacing noise than ever they had made at the height of the anti-English mania. Men called for war—war—war.

It was at this point that private citizen Alexander Hamilton spoke up, making an excellent suggestion. Why not instruct Mr. Pinckney to stay where he was until he could be joined by two fellow Americans, George Cabot and John Marshall, who would be sent immediately, armed, like Pinckney himself, with powers both plenipotentiary and extraordinary? *That* should convince France that we were sincere in our search for peace.

The President agreed, but he did not like the nominations. Both men were stout Federalists, but Cabot was a Tory of Tories, one of Hamilton's most precious "rich and well-born." Adams thought he might substitute for Cabot another Massachusetts man, a friend of *his,* Elbridge Gerry. Gerry too was a Federalist, but not a very convinced one. He had been known to express liberal ideas.

The President called in the Vice President, and they conferred. Jefferson had no objection to Gerry, a man who might have been —and was soon to become—one of his own followers. But he would have preferred James Madison. With the President's permission he asked Madison about it, but Madison declined the honor. Gerry was appointed.

This was the only time that the President conferred with the Vice President.

Hamilton was furious. As far as *he* was concerned, the Presidential honeymoon ended then and there.

The Senate ratified both appointments promptly, and Marshall and a little later Gerry took off to join C. C. Pinckney. The other two did not trust Gerry. For one thing, the mysterious bankers who represented the French foreign minister, Charles Maurice de Talleyrand-Périgord, from the first seemed to favor Gerry above his compatriots almost as though he were a different—and superior —type of man. Probably the bankers did this for the purpose of splitting the delegation, but it should be noted that these men really believed that a large majority of Americans were followers of Thomas Jefferson, who had been held down by the dictatorial methods of George Washington and his successor John Adams. They knew that while all three of the envoys were members of the Federalist party, Pinckney and Marshall were violently anti-Jeffersonian, whereas Gerry was more moderate in his opinions and hence (from their point of view) a truer representative of the American people.

At any rate, after the others withdrew, revolted by the Frenchmen's demand for money, Gerry, feasted and flattered, lingered in France, though he must have known that the High Federalists at home would call this behavior treason, as indeed they did. Elbridge Gerry was a man with a mission. He truly believed that he was single-handedly holding off a war, and it could just be that he was right. To be sure, Pinckney and Marshall resound-

ingly declared to the French diplomats that the United States
was not to be bribed, but Gerry alone may have convinced them
that this country really sought peace.

Of all this the Americans at home knew nothing—for a long
time. When the visitors in Paris started writing their reports to
the Secretary of State, they wrote regularly and at length. However, the sea situation being what it was, their letters went by a
roundabout way, and not until the following spring was a packet
of them handed to Secretary of State Pickering. This was late
afternoon, and by the time Pickering had finished reading such
parts of the letters as had not been put into code, it was late at
night. Nevertheless, and though he certainly was no alarmist, the
secretary called for his hat and cloak and went straight to the
President's $2,700-a-year house, where he caused the President to
be awakened.

The news was amazing. Such of the letters as could be read
that night told of deliberate snubs, of hold-off tactics, of demands
in Talleyrand's name for a *douceur* of 1.2 million livres
($250,000), as well as a "loan" of $12 million from the government of the United States to the French Directory. They told of
threats that the United States would be enslaved as surely as
had been Venice and the Batavian Republic (Holland). They
also told of the Foreign Minister's boast that he could overthrow
the United States government by means of the overwhelmingly
superior political party headed by that friend of France, Thomas
Jefferson.

President Adams, shaken, might or might not have asked Pickering's advice on the spot, instead of waiting for the next regular
Cabinet meeting. If he did, undoubtedly he got a direct answer:
Turn the whole thing over to Congress with a recommendation
of war. Pickering had long been in favor of war anyway.

Ordinarily Pickering would not have answered so promptly.
He would, rather, have conferred with his party chief, which
would take the better part of a week. This was a routine procedure in those early days of the Adams administration, when the

President's Cabinet was not really his own, three quarters of it belonging to Alexander Hamilton.

Determined to carry on Washington's practices as much as possible, Adams had continued the custom of putting large questions to his Cabinet, individually or as a body, and giving them time to submit written opinions. Wolcott and McHenry, like Pickering, always asked Hamilton's advice, by mail, transmitting this advice, often word for word, to the President. But John Adams did not know about this interesting practice at the time the letters from the French mission were handed to him.

What should be done about this devastating report? Should it be made public? Wouldn't that result in an irresistible demand for war? Should the envoys be recalled? Or were they, perhaps, already on their way back? Should Congress be notified, and if so in full? Wouldn't *that* mean war?

It was several days before the cryptographers could complete their work, though the translation, when done at last, proved no more shocking than the English portions of the letters. It was several days more before President Adams decided to turn the whole mess over to Congress, in part because the Republicans had been clamoring for it. The Republicans, having once seen it, wished that they hadn't, which perhaps is what John Adams had in mind; for the publication of these papers touched off an explosion of xenophobia, together with a war scare, the like of which the country had never before known. Suddenly France could do no right, and Gallomen in the streets, in the taverns, most emphatically in the halls of Congress, were chivvied into silence.

The President did not point out that corruption was a way of life in French parliamentary circles of the time; that every other nation in Europe—always with the exception of Great Britain —was being made to pay tribute; that by custom ambassadors to Paris were milked before they were received; that the sensational military victories of the French armies, and especially those of the brilliant young Bonaparte, invariably were followed by cash demands from Paris that could only be called large-scale

bribes. He did not remind the Congressmen that Prince Talleyrand had publicly proclaimed his belief that the world was divided
into two classes, the shearers and the shorn. He did not even point
out that the qualified United States representatives had never been
received, much less consulted, but had rather been snubbed, so-
licited, scolded. He did not need to. The papers themselves did
that.

Adams had taken out only three small things before passing
this material on to Congress—the names of Talleyrand's agents,
the three bankers who had actually extended their palms, crying
"Il faut de l'argent! Il faut beaucoup d'argent!" The three were
Hottenguer, Bellamy, and Hauteval, but the President, for reasons
not apparent today, substituted for their names the letters *X* and
Y and *Z*.

The substitution worked an unintended magic. It lent an air of
European murkiness to the whole matter. It made it seem sinister,
foreign, the doings of despicable, devious men. It made it seem
evil.

The business had been bad enough to begin with. Now, as the
XYZ Affair, it became monstrous.

Pinckney had taken his daughter with him to France. She was
not well and he thought that the sea air of the Riviera might help
her, so he had asked for and been granted an extension of the
time he could spend in that country. Gerry, still being made much
of by Talleyrand himself, still believing that he could somehow
avert war, continued to linger in Paris. Only John Marshall came
right home, and the hero's welcome that he received must have
made him blink in bewilderment, for he was a glum, ungracious
man and not used to public adoration.

A banquet was held in his honor at Oeller's Hotel in Philadelphia. It was attended by 120 guests, all distinguished. Sixteen
toasts were offered at this affair, the thirteenth, the invention of
some anonymous genius, being "Millions for defense, not one cent
for tribute!"

It caught on. In the popular imagination it was attributed to John Marshall himself, though Marshall never pretended that he had said anything of the sort, any more than had Pinckney, much less Elbridge Gerry. The nearest that any of them had come to such a response was Pinckney's startled, and probably stammered, "No, no, not one sixpence!" But that did not have the ring, the swing, of "Millions for defense . . ."

The War Whoopers had a slogan. And they were in the saddle.

★ 16 ★

The Ride of the War Whoopers

★ Things were moving fast. The year 1798 was a busy one in Philadelphia. It had been April 3 when President Adams gave to the House of Representatives the shocking XYZ letters, causing the War Whoop Faction to whoop with delight and stunning many Republicans, who thereafter for a little while stayed away from Congress rather than be called upon to vote for anything that would seem to favor France. A few even went over to the Federalists.

Three weeks before this, however, the President in a message to Congress announced the failure of the negotiations in Paris. He warned the nation that war might be near and called upon the lawmakers to take steps to prepare for it. The Vice President called that message "insane," and even after the XYZ letters had been published, he tried to make men believe that the solicitation of bribes had been the work of "private swindlers" who were "unauthorized" by the French foreign minister. However, only his closest and warmest followers were paying attention to what the Vice President said just then.

Several years before, the building of three first-class frigates had been authorized by Congress, but the proper appropriation had not been made, and the work, although started, had lagged.

Now suddenly the money was voted, and the three ships became realities.

Congress legalized the arming of American merchant vessels. It suspended all commercial intercourse with France and abrogated the 1778 treaties. It authorized the issuance of letters of marque, and the privateers who operated under them were privileged to attack any foreign vessel of war that was acting in a menacing manner off the coast of the United States. The name "France" did not appear in any of these measures, any more than did the word "war," but everybody knew what was meant. Soon the privateering authority was extended to include any vessel anywhere on the high seas, whether or not it was near the United States. Obviously this was meant for the benefit of American privateers who would like to pick up prizes near the French West Indies, though once again the name of France was not used.

Congress appropriated $250,000 for port and harbor defenses and opened negotiations for the purchase from Great Britain of 25,000 muskets and a large number of cannon, both land and naval. The Senate authorized the raising of a "provisional army" of 20,000 men, though the House later cut this to 10,000.

On April 30 the Navy Department was created, and a Maryland merchant, Benjamin Stoddert, its first secretary, was given Cabinet rank.

A few months later, July 11, the Marine Corps, which had gone out of existence when the Continental Navy did, was refounded.

To pay for all this, or at least for much of it, Congress provided for the imposition of a direct tax on "dwelling houses, lands, and slaves."

The tax measure, predictably, was unpopular, but for the rest the public seemed to be right behind the government. The tricolor cockade, which had been seen everywhere during the 1796 campaign, almost disappeared, to be replaced by a black cockade, not so much English in its statement of partisanship as anti-French. The master of Mount Vernon, a private citizen now who was released from his real or imagined duty to refrain from taking sides, burst forth in letters to friends in a startling spate of invective directed against the fellow countrymen of his beloved Marquis de Lafayette, and these philippics of his were much repeated by the common man. Also, the War Whoopers now had not only a slogan but a song.

The New Theater in Philadelphia was *the* place to go, and there, between the acts, the players customarily came out on stage to sing the favorite songs of the day—"Ça Ira," "The Marseillaise," and the like. Publication of the XYZ papers had changed this, so that not applause but a shower of decaying vegetables greeted these French airs, while the house roared for something American—"Yankee Doodle" maybe, or "The President's March." The manager, distressed, in tears, pleaded that there were no *words* to "The President's March."

"Then I'll write some," cried a member of the audience, a young man named Joseph Hopkinson, and he did so, on the spot. The next night, April 25, the most popular member of the company, Gilbert Fox, sang "Hail Columbia, Happy Land!/Hail ye heroes, heav'n-born band!" It was America's first smash hit.

That is the way in which the United States drifted into or was nudged into what historians have called the Quasi-War with France. John Adams knew it as the Half-War. In fact it wasn't a war at all.

It started badly. The Secretary of the Navy, Stoddert, as one of his first acts, endeared himself to the War Whoopers by asking for twelve ships of the line of 74 guns each, twelve frigates, and between twenty and thirty smaller war vessels. This fleet would have made the United States a naval power equal to France, almost a rival to Great Britain, but it was never built. Congress considered the cost first.

Under the despised Articles of Confederation, the United States treasury had found no difficulty in borrowing all the money it needed, in part from the French government, in part from the hardheaded private bankers of Amsterdam, at 5 percent, but now, under the Hamiltonian setup, which was supposed to bolster the country's credit, it had trouble borrowing $5 million at 8 percent. Congress, with this in mind, cut Stoddert's paper fleet to six ships and six sloops. The sloops were to be built, in time. The ships never were.

The three hastily completed frigates that already existed took to sea that summer of 1798, the hopes of all patriotic Americans going with them. It was planned that they should cruise, separately, among the West Indies, where they might pick up some of the pesky French privateers that swarmed in those waters. Largely because of these depredations, marine insurance rates had soared recently.

The *Constellation,* 44 guns, made the cruise but didn't pick up so much as a rowboat. The *Delaware,* only slightly smaller, did catch a French privateer off the coast of New Jersey, but this ship, refitted, manned with Americans, and renamed *Retaliation,* was promptly overtaken by two French warships, to which she struck her flag. The *Constitution,* the pride of the department—the same that was later to be nicknamed Old Ironsides—picked up a privateer too, but it was the wrong kind—a *British* privateer— and had to be returned, with an apology and damages that amounted to $11,000. Then the *Constitution* sprang her bowsprit in a bad blow and had to limp back to Boston for long, expensive repairs, thus ending the first season.

The army did not even do as well as that.

On July 2 President Adams sent to the Senate George Washington's commission as a lieutenant general. The Father of his Country, though he had been titular Commander-in-Chief of the Continental Army throughout the Revolution, and though he had from time to time faced many lieutenant generals in the field—Howe, Clinton, von Knyphausen, Cornwallis—himself had never held a higher rank than that of major general. Now he was promoted. It was understood that he was accepting this commission, together with the new Commander in Chiefship, only on the condition that he would not be expected to serve unless and until a foreign foe actually had invaded the United States of America.

Despite Washington's rather fretful retirement to Mount Vernon, he was still by all odds the most popular personage in the country, and it was believed that his acceptance of the nominal command would attract thousands of sturdy young men to the colors. This was an error.

The regular army numbered about 3,500 at this time, and it was broken into many small garrisons scattered through the wilderness of the West and along the Canadian border. By common consent it would be of no use in the coming war with France, being needed where it was. Nor would the militia suffice. It was the Provisional Army so recently decreed by Congress that George Washington would take command of, and this army had yet to come into being. Ten thousand was the rank-and-file number specified—and authorized—but where were they?

In the old Continental Army colonels had been paid $90 a month, captains $45, privates $7, but because this money had been paid in Continental currency it amounted to $3.30, $1.55, and 26¢, which could not be called princely. The cost of living had gone up since that time, but the regular army was still paid on the old scale, though a few fringe benefits had been added, a few withholding charges eliminated. It was proposed to pay the members of the Provisional Army the same amounts, so there was no rush to the enlistment stands.

With officers it was different. Requests for commissions poured into the War Office, and they all had to be passed upon by the Commander-in-Chief and his staff. But here a very large question obtruded itself: Who would *be* his staff?

Because of Washington's promise that he would not take the field unless there was an invasion, the second-in-command, who would hold the position of inspector general, would be the actual leader of the Provisional Army. There were three applicants for this all-important position, and the first of them, as he was the most clamorous, was Alexander Hamilton.

Hamilton's friends in Congress and the Cabinet kept him informed about what was on the legislative calendar, formally and otherwise, and so it was that a month before the Provisional Army had been authorized he was writing to the ex-President at Mount Vernon asking for the inspector generalship. Nothing less, he made it clear, would induce him to give up, temporarily, his lucrative law practice. Thus he got into the race first, and he had the highest card to play—Washington.

Hamilton was only a brigadier in the reserves. Two other applicants outranked him: Henry Knox and C. C. Pinckney, just back from France. These men were major generals, and Knox's commission was dated earlier than that of Pinckney, which, according to orthodox military reasoning, would place him at the top of the list. That, exactly, was the way the distinguished civilian, John Adams, proposed to send the commissions to Congress: Knox, Pinckney, Hamilton.

But Adams reckoned without his own Cabinet. Wolcott and Pickering both wrote to the Sage of Mount Vernon, Pickering repeatedly. McHenry not only wrote, he also went there. As a result, the lieutenant general wrote to the Secretary of War, giving him a list of his staff in the order of their seniority as *he* saw it. It was exactly the reverse of Adams' list: Hamilton, Pinckney, Knox.

The Battle of the Generals was joined.

The President was embarrassed, but even if you were President, you didn't refuse to obey an order from George Washington, especially at a time of public fright. The President proposed to send the three names to Congress in no particular order and let that body list them as it thought best, but Washington, warned by McHenry, coldly put a stop to this. Washington said that if he couldn't name his own assistants he would not serve as Commander-in-Chief. The President said yes, sir, and did as he was told. It was a scalding humiliation.

The President did make one further effort to assert his authority as Constitutional Commander-in-Chief. His party, the Federalists, had been flirting with the dashing young Revolutionary veteran Aaron Burr, whose talents for political organization, especially in cities, it could surely use, and Burr's military rank and record were at least equal to those of Alexander Hamilton. Adams therefore proposed to appoint Burr to the *fifth* highest post in the Provisional Army, a brigadiership. This proposal was vetoed, not by Washington but by the inspector general, who didn't like Burr.

These somewhat Central American doings were watched by an apprehensive citizenry, for the war scare was a very real one, and many a man in America, forgetting the constant presence of the British navy in the Atlantic Ocean, feared that French bayonets would soon glint along our shoreline and French jackboots tread our village greens. After that, what? What would happen to us when the hated atheists had taken over our land? Worse, what would happen to our womenfolk? The Reverend Timothy Dwight, president of Yale and a doughty Federalist, had an answer to this last question. Our wives and daughters under French rule, he warned his congregation, might become "the victims of legal prostitution . . . speciously polluted." Many, many believed this.

John Adams was not one of them. "There is no more chance of seeing a French army here than there is in Heaven," he wrote to Secretary McHenry.

John Adams kept working for peace, but he had to work quietly. He had promised Congress, passionately, that he would not appoint another ambassador to Paris until he had received "assurances that he will be received, respected, and honored as the representative of a great, free, powerful, and independent nation." Yet he had to be careful to keep his speeches angry, lest the public turn against him, and undeniably he was pleased, this lonesome man, by the popularity that was suddenly his, so much louder, so much more sincere, it seemed, than the popularity that had been granted him at the time of the Presidential honeymoon. Now he was being cheered when he entered a theater, a new experience. He was even cheered in the towns he passed through on his way back and forth between Philadelphia and Braintree, Massachusetts, to visit Abigail, who was ailing and should not be exposed to the unhealthy air of Philadelphia. The *Vomito Negro* had broken out again in the capital, and so the President spent much of his time with her on the family farm, nine months at a stretch once.

Why then did Alexander Hamilton go into this thing so fervently? He was too intelligent and well informed a man to suppose that there was any chance of a French invasion, and yet it cannot be thought that he would interrupt a career at the New York bar in order to raise and equip and train an army (though it was a job for which he was supremely well fitted) that would never be called upon to fight. To him war was battle, not the addition and subtraction of figures, not the ordering of supplies. He still thought of himself as racing against the foe, his sword brandished high, while all the world gasped in admiration. Why then did he seek a command that could only mean, in the ordinary course of events, desk work and then more desk work, the disposal of unexciting details?

The answer was Sebastian Francisco Miranda.

This was a young man of Caracas, who had served with the French in the American Revolution. That particular conflict over, he looked about for an army at the head of which he could free the rest of America, beginning, of course, with his own homeland of Venezuela.

Spain, clearly, was on a decline. She couldn't continue to hold all of the New World that she had grabbed in her heyday. Miranda was well connected and made a good appearance, and soon he was to be seen in most of the European capitals, one after the other. From each of these he was expelled, usually at the request of the Spanish ambassador, but expelled with gifts, with an invitation to return any time he saw fit. Foreign ministers thought that Francisco Miranda might be a good thing to have around if ever it happened that the circumstances were just right, and they liked to hope that they could get him whenever they called, even though they could not afford him right now.

In this capacity Miranda visited the United States again, an honored veteran. John Adams, who had just been inaugurated as the second President, saw him, but was cool, noncommittal. Miranda then called upon Alexander Hamilton, who was even more cool. Hamilton dismissed him, in letters to friends, as "an intriguing adventurer."

Things were different now, however. Miranda was being taken up in London, where he hobnobbed with Pitt the Younger and other important persons, and where there just might be a movement to back him. Certainly the time was ripe for a dismemberment of Latin America. Spain was an ally, if not a very enthusiastic one, of France, but France, what with the British navy, was in no position to help Spain protect her weak American colonies. What a market *they* would make! Spain had kept them to herself too long.

Great Britain, in the course of that fit of absentmindedness during which she conquered half the world, often had done things as bold as this. She had the ships. What she lacked was the men, the soldiers. Could not the United States be persuaded to supply them, being offered in return the Floridas, perhaps even Mexico? They were talking about it in London.

Hamilton heard of this through the United States ambassador there, his good friend Rufus King, and he saw it as his opportunity! *He* of course would be the leader of the American expeditionary force, the conqueror of Florida, New Orleans, Mexico! All that was needed was that Provisional Army, for which funds had already been allocated. He went to work with a will, and Knox, angry, resigned, refusing to serve under the man he had already given the best years of his political life.

Hamilton, Washington, and Charles Cotesworth Pinckney spent almost a month in Philadelphia—from ten to three every day, from seven to nine thirty every night—screening applications for commissions. This was necessary because there were believed to be some among them that came from members of the Republican-Democratic party, and these, of course, had to be weeded out. Hamilton did suggest a few times that some of the less radical Republican applicants might be admitted to officerdom, for if they were exposed long enough to right thinkers, it could convert them. But Washington remained obdurate, declaring "that you could as soon scrub a blackamore white as to change the principles of a professed Democrat; and that he will leave nothing unattempted to overturn the Government of this country."

The year 1798 closed sadly for the War Whoopers. France was not advancing any more insults and at times even appeared to be willing to talk things over. General Hamilton had learned through his London pipelines that the British had no thought of backing a Miranda expedition that was not under the complete command of their own officers, army and naval, with the Americans as a mere subservient ally, a hanger-on force. With this the inspector general lost interest. Unless they made him captain of the team, he would not play ball. Anyway, what would he have led? Even his managerial energy and skill could not create an army where there were no soldiers.

The American navy, after a flabby start, was making itself felt in Caribbean waters. The vessels it picked up were virtually all small French privateers—a total of eighty-four of them in the two and a half years that the Half-War was to last—but the work did help to bring insurance rates down a bit. Then, on February 9 of the new year, there came a first-class victory to cheer American hearts. The U.S.S. *Constellation,* a frigate, under Commodore Thomas Truxtun, encountered a French frigate, *L'Insurgente,* a vessel of about her own size and gunnage. She instantly attacked, and within half an hour the Frenchman was seen to strike its flag.

Otherwise, however, all the news was discouraging. Miranda's plots were not known to most Americans, many of whom quite naturally assumed that Alexander Hamilton's eagerness to get command of the army meant that he hoped to use it to implant

permanently upon the nation his own rich man's form of government, crushing out every trace of states' rights. Many Americans
too, like many Frenchmen, seemed to be growing tired of this
transoceanic bickering, which was getting neither side anywhere.

It looked, in short, as though any day now peace might rear
its ugly head.

★ 17 ★

"You Will Have No War!"

★ All this while the Federalist party was cutting its own throat. It might be supposed that so spectacular an act would be performed in a spectacular fashion, but the Federalists were quiet about it, or tried to be, and whatever noise was raised was raised by the protesting Republicans.

The Federalists, it must be remembered, never had accepted the existence of a two-party system. They regarded all who differed with them in matters political as, quite simply, traitors. Opposition was never legitimate, never natural.

This applied as much to newspapers as to persons. The semi-official *Gazette of the United States* made the matter perfectly clear in its October 10, 1798, number: "It is Patriotism to write in favor of our government—it is sedition to write against it."

The High Federalists of the late 1700's can be compared with the Republican Old Guard of today, for though they might die, they would never surrender. In their own time they were called Bourbons. It was said that they never learned anything and never forgot anything.

They were afflicted with a severe case of xenophobia, and this too must be borne in mind when the attempted self-decapitation mentioned above is taken under examination. They hated foreigners in any form. Uriah Tracy of Connecticut, one of the first of the secessionists, was not being irreverent when he spoke of "the most God-provoking Democrats this side of Hell," and an extremely high High Federalist, Harrison Gray Otis of Massachusetts, meant every word of it when he said that "if some means are not adopted to prevent the indiscriminate admission of wild Irishmen and others to the rights of suffrage, there will soon be an end to liberty and property."

A law of 1790 permitted naturalization of the foreigner after two years of residence in the United States. Another law, in 1795, raised the time to five years. The Naturalization Act of 1798 raised it to *fourteen.*

Other limiting proposals failed to squeak through, such as the proposal advanced by Harrison Gray Otis and Robert Goodloe Harper that the Constitution be amended to deny the vote to all persons not born in the United States, no matter how long their residence here, or the bill that provided that all aliens, whether naturalized or not, should be forbidden to teach school or to edit newspapers.

It was natural, in the circumstances, that newcomers to the United States preferred the political party that didn't hate them. They became Republican-Democrats.

Much of the Federalists' antiforeigners fury was directed, at first, against the corrupt journalists from Ireland, Scotland, and England, who came to this country prepared to sell their spitefulness to the highest bidder. However, the pet abomination of the rich and the well-born, their *bête noire,* was a young man who had been born in Switzerland and spoke English with a heavy German accent.

Albert Gallatin came from an aristocratic family, but his feelings were all for the underdog. He could not be called, even by the Anglomen, a Galloman; yet the Tory instincts were sound that called for his harpooning, for along with James Madison he did as much as any non-Federalist to bring about the wreck of the Federalist party.

Gallatin had dabbled in trade and in land speculation, neither very successfully, and he taught at Harvard for a little while. He married Hannah Nicholson, the daughter of Commodore James Nicholson, a union that might have admitted him to the ranks of the chosen few had he been so bent, but he refrained. He lived in western Pennsylvania, near the Virginia line, and at the time of the Whiskey Insurrection, he was openly on the side of those who opposed the excise tax, though never guilty of sedition. He was elected to the United States Senate, much to the disgust of the other Senators, who after a while managed to expel him on the technical ground that his election had been illegal because he had not been a naturalized resident of Pennsylvania for nine years at the time. He was then elected to the House of Representatives, where he came into his own.

He brought about the establishment of the House Ways and Means Committee, which quickly became—as it still is today—the most powerful committee in Congress. He was its first chairman. He instituted the system of regulated appropriations, giving so-and-so-much money for this-and-that purpose instead of simply dumping large lump sums upon various executive departments to be distributed when and as the sundry Secretaries saw fit. This system, which is still in use today, not only saved money but increased the Congressional control of these funds. Had the system been in operation from the beginning, it would have prevented Alexander Hamilton from getting such a head start in the push for power.

Gallatin indeed could be compared with Hamilton, for he too was undeniably a financial wizard. Undeniably too he was, like Hamilton, honest. The Federalists jeered at his accent, his pronunciation of "we have" as "ve haff" and so forth, but they were obliged to admit that he did a good job.

He was one of the unsung heroes of early American politics.

The Alien and Sedition Acts were four in number, though they are usually written of and were thought of in their time as one or at most two.

The first was the Naturalization Act, extending the residence requirement to fourteen years. This might have been thought unwise—it was unmistakably a political move, designed to keep the Republican-Democratic party from becoming even more powerful—but probably it was not unconstitutional.

Then there were two Alien acts, a friendly one and an enemy one. The so-called Friendly Alien Act was largely aimed at the recent arrivals from Ireland—always referred to as the Wild Irish—but it was widely interpreted by the recently arrived French to be directed at them, so that they began to leave the country in large numbers. Most of them never had meant to stay in the United States long anyway, only until things in France grew more settled.

This Act gave the President extraordinary powers, authorizing him to order out of the country "such aliens as he shall judge dangerous to the peace and safety of the United States or shall have reasonable grounds to suspect are concerned in any treasonable or secret machinations against the government thereof."

Then there was the so-called Enemy Alien Act, which definitely *was* directed against the Frenchmen in America, and permitted the executive department to do just about anything it wished with them. This was a wartime measure, and was meant as nothing less, and the fact that the United States was not at war with France did not bother the Federalists, who were betting everything on the bringing about of such a war.

Finally, and worst of all, was the Sedition Act. It was clearly unconstitutional. It branded as a traitor, punishable by two to five years in jail or a fine of $5,000 or both, "any person, whether alien or citizen, who shall . . . openly combine with an intention of opposing any measures of the Government of the United States." There was more, all bad. Any person who "shall write, print, utter, or publish . . . any false, scandalous, and malicious writing or writings against the Government of the United States, or either House of Congress of the United States, or the President of the United States . . ." could be jailed for two years and fined $2,000.

All of this, of course, was done in the name of the national security.

In England, the Federalists were to point out, even stricter naturalization and libel laws were in effect. But England was at war. The French, on their side of the Channel, were openly preparing boats for an invasion. Only the previous spring the Bank of England, desperate, had suspended payments. Government bonds were at their lowest in history. Ireland recently had been in revolt again. There had been naval mutinies at the Nore and at Spithead that involved 50,000 men and 113 war vessels, so that for a little while the overstrained Royal Navy, upon which the very existence of the islands depended, was threatened with dissolution, extinction.

Americans faced no such emergency. American backs were not against a wall. France had been arrogant, insolent, yes, and France had been quarrelsome, but with all the nations of Europe in her own front yard, spoiling for an excuse to break out of a hated captivity, even mad-dog France was not about to declare war upon her best source of supplies, three thousand miles away. Only the High Federalists of the United States really sought war, and they wanted it as a threat, not as the real thing.

The Sedition Act was pointed at the editors of the Philadelphia *Aurora,* the Richmond *Examiner,* the New York *Argus,* and the *Independent Chronicle* of Boston, men who had dared to find fault, often impolitely, with the way the Federalists were running the country. The Act could blast these men out of business, scaring off all others.

President Adams, though he had sent a strongly worded "war message" to Congress just before he submitted to that body the XYZ papers, and though he had signed the Alien and Sedition Acts as they came to him, did not wait in Philadelphia for the expected declaration of hostilities but hurried off to Braintree and to Abigail.

Seated in the chair of impotence as presiding officer of the United States Senate, which was something between 2½ and 3 to 1 Federalist, Vice President Jefferson did nothing to check the rush of laws that could change the whole nature of the United States. There was nothing he could have done. The fight, such as it was, was in the House, where Livingston and Gallatin and Madison toiled valiantly but in vain. Jefferson did deplore, and bitterly, the fact that there were ten Republican absentees when the House passed the worst measure of them all, the Sedition bill, by a mere 45 to 41. The House ordinarily split 52–54 or else 51–55.

Thereafter, and a couple of weeks before the Congress was scheduled to adjourn, Jefferson went back to Monticello, where he framed a set of resolutions declaring, in effect, that any state had the right and even the duty to brand as undesirable any law that it thought violated the "compact" of the Constitution, and to set it aside. It did not call for any manner of rebellion. It did not even mention the Alien and Sedition Acts.

Jefferson did not sign this paper, and did not even acknowledge authorship, though neither did he deny it. He believed, with good reason, that if his name were connected with it, at just that time, it would ruin the thing. Instead, he persuaded John Breckinridge, Speaker of the Kentucky House, to present it to that body as his own. He then persuaded James Madison to do the same thing in Virginia, using as his spokesman the eminent Virginian democratic theoretician, John Taylor of Caroline. Madison's resolutions were similar to Jefferson's though not so belligerent in tone. Both were passed by large majorities, almost unanimously, the Kentucky Resolutions in November of 1798, the Virginia Resolutions in December.

Neither Madison nor Jefferson was a secretive man, and neither was sneaky. The reason for the use of go-betweens was because they knew that just then their own names would have made a party matter of it, and they wished it to be placed squarely before the people with no partisan strings attached, no partisan shadow thrown. Each legislature sent copies of the resolutions to the governors of all the states, asking for an informal ratification.

It was a bold idea, but it fell flat. Most of the governors refused even to consider the matter; others failed to reply. Not one endorsed the resolutions.

Nevertheless the Kentucky and Virginia resolutions, though immediately a flop, were in time to lead to John C. Calhoun's momentous nullification theory—and so to the Civil War. There were to be secession threats still from New England, but from that time on, the issue belonged predominantly to the South.

There were many reasons why the resolutions did not cause a stir. The War Whoopers were still loud in the land, and if they got their way, if they succeeded in bringing about a declaration of hostilities, then the Republican-Democratic party would be crushed, Hamilton would get his army, and the United States would cease to be free.

Hamilton indeed did seize this opportunity to do a little saber rattling. Disappointed in the Miranda venture, he looked upon Virginia as a possible subject for punishment, an example, as the western Pennsylvania counties had been in 1794. Perhaps, to make everything safe for Federalism, he should march now? There were many who feared that he would, using his private army. But—that army still refused to materialize. Officers, yes; men, no.

What's more, there were glimmers of light now on the French situation.

Gerry had returned, to be a pariah among Federalists. There was still no official contact with the Quai d'Orsay, but from Amsterdam William Vans Murray and from London Rufus King reported that Talleyrand was showing a genuine wish to talk peace and a willingness to treat with any duly accredited envoy from "a great, free, powerful, and independent nation" such as the United States. Moreover, the international scene had undergone a radical change. France had suffered some bad defeats in the field, and her Mediterranean fleet had been wiped out at Aboukir. She no longer threatened an invasion of the British Isles. The Directory, rotten, was wobbling, and the Bourbon pretender, it seemed, was poised for a comeback.

At the same time Dr. George Logan returned to the United States. Logan was a Quaker from Philadelphia who was, like his friend Thomas Jefferson, a scientific farmer. He was also a sincere if unofficial seeker after peace, and he had gone to France of his own accord, at his own expense, to see Talleyrand. On his return he got an audience with Timothy Pickering, who was still Secretary of State. Pickering was one of the highest of the High Federalists, a disagreeable man who sometimes thought that he was God. He listened in silence to the Quaker's earnest story, and then opened the door for him. "Sir, it is my duty to inform you that the government does not thank you for what you have done," he said.

Because of this, Congress, soon afterward, passed the so-called Logan Law, which provided that any citizen who shall "without the permission or authority of the Government of the United States, directly or indirectly, commence or carry on, any verbal or written correspondence or intercourse with any foreign Government, or any officer or agent thereof, in relation to any disputes or controversies with the United States" shall be deemed guilty of a high misdemeanor punishable by fine *and* imprisonment. This law is still on the books. As recently as the spring of 1947 the late and unlamented J. Parnell Thomas, speaking for the unspeakable House Un-American Activities Committee, tried to prosecute Henry Wallace under it.

Suddenly, unexpectedly, President Adams sent to Congress a message proposing that three ambassadors be dispatched to France in order to arrange a nonpeace to end the nonwar.

The shock of this was stupendous. Adams had not conferred with his Cabinet or with anybody else, so that even Alexander Hamilton did not know about it, while Pickering was driven almost mad. The Federalist leaders were already worried about the failure of the Provisional Army to solidify and the flood of protests against the Alien and Sedition Acts. They looked askance at the seriousness with which their own Rufus King in London was taking the French advances toward a talk—"You will have no war!" he had written to Hamilton—and at the numbers of otherwise respectable persons who seemed to think that

Elbridge Gerry and Dr. Logan were honest men honestly striving to keep their country from the brink of disaster. The Federalist leaders truly seemed to believe that the President had done a stupid, rash thing, a *dishonorable* thing.

Adams was unperturbed. He might even have enjoyed the rage with which his action had been greeted.

For head of this proposed mission Adams nominated William Vans Murray, who did not need to be sent, for he was already on the scene, more or less. He was a young man, a Federalist but no fanatic, the United States ambassador to the Netherlands, stationed in Amsterdam. He had not approved of Gerry's or of Logan's activity in Paris, but his disapproval had been largely based on professional, bureaucratic grounds. Also, he could speak French.

The President then asked Oliver Ellsworth to serve, and he agreed. He was the Chief Justice of the Supreme Court.

The next to be asked was Patrick Henry, and he, fortunately, refused. That irascible old ex-radical would have been the worst ambassador in the world. Adams substituted for his name that of William R. Davie, governor of North Carolina, and he accepted.

As soon as these names cleared the Senate, President Adams, who had been worrying about Abigail, departed for Braintree. He was to be gone for many months, and during that time Pickering and his partners on one pretext or another made every effort to block the sailing of Ellsworth and Davie, without whom William Vans Murray could not function in France. They were clearly desperate, and they took every advantage of the President's absence. Adams, for his part, though his friends begged him to return, kept insisting that he could run the government perfectly well from Massachusetts.

When at last John Adams did leave his beloved Braintree, it was not to go back to Philadelphia but to Trenton, New Jersey, because another yellow fever epidemic was raging in the Quaker City, almost as bad as the one of 1793, and Congress and the various government departments had shifted their working quarters.

In Trenton, amazingly, Adams was met by no less a person than Alexander Hamilton, who had come all the way from New York to explain the situation to him.

Hamilton knew, probably even better than did his man Pickering, that if that two thirds of a delegation sailed, all hope of war would be gone. It was the High Federalists' golden opportunity, now that they had the Alien and Sedition laws, and had the entire federal bench under their control, to stamp out the opposition party. They could do this only if they had a war. Not a *fighting* war, perhaps, but at least a *declared* war.

That was why Hamilton took over in person. He explained to the President how the peace mission should be canceled, and why. He "exhausted" the subject, lawyerlike. He waggled his finger, dismayed to see that the President, though silent, clearly disagreed. "He marveled at the pertinacity with which the old man persisted in error and resisted enlightenment," wrote historian John C. Miller. Hamilton labored mightily, but he did not prevail.

Afterward the stubborn chief magistrate ordered the two ambassadors-designate, who had been waiting for months, their chests packed, to be on their way.

At about this time, too, John Adams learned about the strings Hamilton had attached to the members of his Cabinet and about what had been going on behind his back not just while he was in Braintree but ever since he had been President. He reacted characteristically. He asked McHenry and Pickering to resign. McHenry meekly did so, but Pickering refused. Thereupon the President wrote, very briefly, to the Secretary of State: "Dear sir: You are hereby discharged."

Adams then appointed Samuel ("Ambi") Dexter to War. To State he appointed John Marshall, a High Federalist who, however, disapproved of the Alien and Sedition Acts. The President never did find out about Wolcott's link to Hamilton. He went right on taking orders from and giving inside information to the former Secretary of the Treasury.

Even while the new ambassadors were crossing the Atlantic, the French Directory fell. But it did not fall, as predicted, to the forces of a Bourbon pretender. It fell, rather, to a brand-new revolutionary combination, a three-man consulate, which had used military means to become all powerful. The First Consul was the sensational little general from Corsica, Napoleon Bonaparte.

This marked the end of all show of republicanism in France. It did not ruin the American mission. On the contrary, it helped it. Bonaparte despised Talleyrand (*"De la merde dans un bas de soie"*), but he knew ability when he saw it, and this particular ability, diplomacy, was one of the very few talents he himself lacked. So he bade Talleyrand stay on as Foreign Minister, and Talleyrand, still the assiduous crook, did. The American matter was near at hand, so Talleyrand settled it, being glad to waive his customary rake-off in order to show his new master what he could do.

In an amazingly short time Davie and Ellsworth (Murray stayed on in Europe) were sailing back, having arranged an excellent convention with France. As King had predicted, Hamilton would not get his war, and all of the pyromaniacal efforts of the Federalists had been in vain. The President was to stipulate, years afterward, that all he wanted for an epitaph was: "Here lies John Adams, who took upon himself the responsibility of peace with France in the year 1800."

★ 18 ★

Big-City Doings

★ George Washington died on December 14, 1799, just a few days after the new Congress convened, a few weeks before the turn of the century. The death was not altogether unexpected, though it had been preceded by only a couple of weeks' illness, during which physicians had bled the poor man almost white, and it had no effect upon the makeup of the government or on governmental policies.

There were many memorial services; cannons were fired; white horses with reversed saddles were marched very slowly at the head of slow parades; federal buildings were draped; and of course there were resolutions of sorrow without number. It is remarkable, however, that the middle and Southern states made much less formal fuss about their bereavement than did the New England states, where the keening was loud and prolonged. Washington had always disliked the "leveling" New Englanders, whom he distrusted, but they were Federalists, and they knew that it was their duty to weep.

There was not much else that the Federalists could do, though they did try to capitalize on the dead leader's name by calling the Federalist party—which never had been officially so titled anyway—the Washington party, themselves the Washingtonians. These

efforts failed. The first President's politics were allowed to die
with him.

Politics, however, was everywhere else. It tingled in the air.
It took over the taverns and boardinghouses, and it teemed
through the streets.

The 1796 election for a President had been unexpectedly
close—a mere 3 votes—and there was every indication that the
1800 election would be closer still, and more exciting. Americans
for the first time were looking forward to that quadrennial Big
Show, that obstreperous circus. They were beginning to love it.
Statesmen might sneer, as all statesmen did in those times, at "the
vile practice of electioneering," which often seemed to lead to a
fight, but there was nothing that Americans enjoyed so much as
a good fight. The election of 1800 promised to be just that.

There is much muttering today about the unconscionably long
time that American Presidential campaigns last, and certainly
they are longer and more distracting—and much, *much* more expensive—than the national political campaigns of any other country. Yet in the first days of the republic they were longer still.
This one, for instance, was to last, for all practical purposes,
the whole year.

There were sixteen states, and so there were sixteen different
ways of electing or appointing electors, at sixteen different times.
The laws of suffrage differed from state to state, but in any event
only about one free adult white man out of six could vote. There
was no one "Election Day." Every state fixed its own, and though
it was agreed that the electors should meet and should cast their
votes on December 7, it took a long time after that to learn who,
if anybody—for it might prove to be a tie—had been made
President.

Both parties held caucuses, the first time this distinctively
American political institution had been used on a national scale.
Both parties anxiously scanned the skies for signs of a storm. It
was a year, by general consent, in which almost anything might
happen.

Electors were to be popularly elected in Rhode Island, Maryland, Virginia, North Carolina, and Kentucky. In each of the
other eleven states the electors would be appointed, so that the
fight was for control of the legislature.

There were pockets of Federalism in Virginia, where James
Monroe was now governor, but the Democrat-Republicans put
through a unit-plan law that would make the state safe, in its
entirety, for their candidates. Virginia had 19 electoral votes, the
most. Of the rest of the South, South Carolina was the only soft
spot, as the Republicans saw it. The owners of very large planta-
tions and the trading interests in Charleston, an important port,
made for a large Federalist minority. The party leaders no doubt
had this in mind when they put the name of a South Carolinian,
Charles Cotesworth Pinckney, on the ticket with their own John
Adams.

The former Secretary of the Treasury had still further plans
for Mr. Pinckney. He hoped to persuade whatever Federalist
electors might be elected in South Carolina to vote for Pinckney
only, not Pinckney and Adams, thus ensuring the election (if
the Federalists won) for C. C. Pinckney rather than for John
Adams, the regular candidate. The fact that a similar plan tried
in 1796 had exploded in his face did not faze Hamilton. Hamilton
hated and distrusted Adams, who had declared himself to be his
own man by tossing Hamilton's spies out of the Cabinet, and he
especially hated him since the peace mission had been sent to
France.

There were many Federalists who did not like John Adams,
for the party was badly split, but to fail to renominate him for
the Presidency would be unthinkable. New England, at least,
remained firm behind him.

New England, of course, had been a Federalist stronghold
from the beginning. Aaron Burr, early in that year of 1800, had
made a sweeping visit to the New England states (Maine was
still part of Massachusetts then), interviewing men who might be
in a position to know, and when he came back he reported to
the Republican party leaders that one of those states, little Rhode

Island, an enclave of cantankerousness, an ornery place, ever the home of the otherwise-minded, might—just *might*—go Republican. This cheered the followers of Jefferson, as it depressed the Adamsites, for Burr was a practical, knowledgeable man, and no windbag. However, Rhode Island had only 2 electoral votes.

The South and New England, then, balanced one another, so that it looked as though the middle states—Pennsylvania, New Jersey, New York—would tell the tale.

New Jersey had always been in the Federalist column. It was safe.

Pennsylvania, with its hordes of Irish immigrants, and with such able political organizers as Dallas, Gallatin, and Mifflin, had for years now been a happy hunting ground for the forces of democracy, and Pennsylvania had 15 electoral votes, the second highest number after Virginia. However, the conservatives were well dug in. They had been retreating, but they still controlled the state senate by 2 votes, which might be enough to block the whole delegation to the Electoral College. The Federalists could not hope to *win* in Pennsylvania, where an overwhelming majority of the legislators—not to mention the people themselves —favored the Republican cause, but if they could bring about a stalemate by means of those two stubborn senators, it would amount to a Federalist victory.

New York, by general agreement, would be the pivotal state.

New York, together with New Hampshire and Massachusetts, would vote for electors in the spring. They would be the first.

New Hampshire, rock-solid, gave its 6 electoral votes to the Federalist party. Nobody had expected anything else.

Massachusetts turned in another Federalist victory, but it was a victory that brought great joy to the Republicans, who regarded it as the first crack in the surface, hitherto smooth, of New England Federalism. Elbridge Gerry, never a popular politician, had been virtually read out of his own party and had been persuaded to run for governor on the Republican-Democratic ticket. His opponent, the regular Federalist candidate, was Caleb Strong, who should have been a shoo-in. The result: Strong 19,690,

Gerry 17,019, scattered 2,410. Massachusetts had 14 electoral votes.

New York had 12 electoral votes, and the electors were named by the legislature. There was to be a new legislature elected at large late in April and early in May of that turn-point year 1800, and it would be controlled, as it always was, by the New York City delegation. Alexander Hamilton was the absolute boss in the city. He could name any list of legislative candidates he chose, and he did. He did not pick men for their names, for their families or fortunes. He picked men he knew he could control, now and all the while they might serve in Albany. In his law work he often needed an obedient legislature, and the fact that these candidates were unknowns did not bother him, for he believed their election to be a sure thing anyway.

Hamilton's opposite number, the Republican-Democratic leader, was quiet-spoken Aaron Burr. Burr at this time enjoyed a dazzling reputation as a political wonder-worker. It was due in part to his secretive, knowing manner and his habit of keeping his mouth shut, but it was also due in part to his handling of the Manhattan Company matter.

Though the number of banks in the republic was growing, largely because of the impetus given to them by the establishment of Hamilton's Bank of the United States, there were still only two in New York, both of them Federalist. In the days before the secret ballot was introduced, together with the polling booth, a voter's choice was a public thing. He was asked, aloud, how he would vote, and he answered, aloud, in the presence of a large number of men, some of them representatives of the two banks, who took everything down. If he was a small tradesman, as so often he was in New York City in 1800, he voted Federalist, because if he didn't, if he had the temerity to vote for the disorganizers, the dirty, atheistic democrats, God help him the next time he needed to borrow money or to have a note renewed.

The Federalists were frank about it. They controlled the wealth of the city and the state, and they saw no reason why they should not use this control as a club with which to batter the opposition.

Clearly the thing to do was to liberalize the election laws and set up a bank that would be independent of the Federalist party and responsive to the unpropertied. But none of this could be done without the state legislature, and the legislature was controlled by the Federalists—or at least, it always had been.

When Aaron Burr applied to the legislature at Albany for a charter for his client, the Manhattan Company, he met with no suspicion. Sure, the fellow was one of those democrats, but he was a bona fide lawyer, and the Manhattan Company was a bona fide water company. New York City certainly needed such a company, for the public water there, most of it from the Collect Pond, stank. So why not give the man his charter? It would be a good thing.

The legislators, however, had failed to do what most lawyers loudly demand that their clients *always* do; they failed to read the fine print at the bottom of the page. So it was that they missed this clause:

And be it further enacted, That it shall and may be lawful for the said company to employ all such surplus capital as may belong or accrue to the said company in the purchase of public or other stock, or in any other monied transactions or operations not inconsistent with the constitution and laws of this state or of the United States, for the sole benefit of the said company.

Even a layman could see that this authorized the establishment of a bank, and was in fact a charter, in case the new company had any "surplus capital." And you may be sure that the new company did. Almost as soon as the Manhattan Company began to supply water to the residents of New York City the Bank of the Manhattan Company (which still operates, though the parent concern has long since withered away) began to supply cash loans to citizens who wished to be able to vote free from pressure.

It was all perfectly legal, all open and aboveboard. Nevertheless, the Federalists raised hell. They accused the New York City Republican-Democratic organization, and specifically Aaron Burr, of playing dirty, un-American tricks in that they interfered with the Federalists' coercion of voters. This got them nowhere.

Burr now turned his attention to the task of assembling a strong slate of legislative candidates. He had noted the weakness of Hamilton's slate, and he did just the opposite; he got good men.

This task was not easy. He started with the hardest part of it— George Clinton. The crusty ex-governor did not like Burr, and he certainly did not see why he should serve in the legislature again. Burr had to argue long and low, turning on every bit of the celebrated charm, but at last he got the old man's grudging consent. The rest was thus made easier, though it still called for plenty of persuasion. He went after and in time signed up a set of men who in ordinary circumstances would not even have considered letting their names be used—General Horatio Gates, John Swartout, Brockholst Livingston, Samuel Osgood, Henry Rogers, Elias Nexen, Thomas Storm, George Warner, Philip I. Arcularius, James Hunt, Ezekiel Robins.

Then he made a list of all the legal voters in New York City, though there were more than three thousand of them. He card-indexed these names and personally called upon all who might be in doubt.

His methods were legitimate. He copied no names from tombstones. He employed no shoulder-hitters to patrol the polling places.

New York State had the strictest property requirements for voting in the Union, but Burr smiled—he had never been known to laugh aloud—at this hurdle. He placed on record a series of joint-tenancy deeds to parcels of land just sufficiently large to come within the franchise qualifications. There were from ten to twenty names on each deed, and since the law at that time held that every joint-tenant owned the entire piece of land, all of these became, willy-nilly, voters. Again, it was all perfectly legal. But—nobody had ever thought of it before.

It is possible that in the gathering of names for these title deeds Aaron Burr was assisted in part by some of the members of the Society of St. Tammany and Columbian Order, but to call him, as so many historians have, the "organizer" and "the first boss" of Tammany Hall is ridiculous.

The Society of St. Tammany in New York—there were others of the same name in Brooklyn, Providence, Philadelphia, Lexington —was a social group in 1800 with no political overtones. It had no "boss" and needed none. It had been organized only a few years back, in 1789, and was one of the "self-created democratic societies" that had survived President Washington's attack. It consisted largely of recent arrivals to the United States, or the sons of such newcomers, though it was not then, as it later became, overwhelmingly Irish in its nature. It had been named after an Indian, a Leni-Lenape (Delaware) chieftain, and it affected, rather laboriously, Indian names and Indian manners. Its officers were called sachems and sagamoors, its doorkeeper was a wiskinskie. Its members met once or twice every moon, greeting one another with "Ugh!" and "How!" and "Me know you!" On Independence Day every year they got into aboriginal costumes, more or less, and paraded.

This was the principal reason for their existence. They took no part, collectively or otherwise, in politics. The society's first home had been the long room at Barden's Tavern, but by 1800 it was meeting at Abraham Martling's place at Nassau and Spruce streets, which the members called the Wigwam. Others called it the Pig Pen. Almost certainly Aaron Burr never visited it. Why should he? He was a gentleman.

"Election Day" in New York was in fact three days—April 29, April 30, and May 1. Alexander Hamilton, alarmed when he heard that the Republicans had organized every ward and aware that his ticket was a weak one compared with theirs, spent those three days going from one polling place to another on a white horse. He made a speech at each place, but it did no good. Burr and his trained lieutenants got out the vote, as planned, and they won a smashing success.

Burr did not gloat. He never did. But he went into conference with Thomas Jefferson at Monticello, and he demanded not only the second place on the ballot but also a guarantee that he would get all votes that the leader got in the South. Burr had been Jefferson's running mate in 1796, but he had lost many votes in Jefferson's own state of Virginia, where some Republican-Democrats had either written in only one name or had voted for Jefferson and some other Republican. This had embarrassed Mr. Burr, who wanted to make sure that such a thing would not happen again. Jefferson assured him that it would not, and the Republican caucus designated Aaron Burr to share the ticket with Thomas Jefferson, which was no more than he deserved.

Hamilton? He was a bad loser. He sat down and wrote an extraordinary letter to the governor, his friend John Jay. He proposed that the governor call a special session of the legislature—a lame-duck legislature—and induce it to rewrite the law, making the election of electors a matter for the people at large. In other words, after losing the game he wanted to change the rules and then go back and play it over.

In times like these in which we live [he explained], it will not do to be over scrupulous. It is easy to sacrifice the interests of society by a strict adherence to ordinary rules . . . the scruples of delicacy and propriety, as relative to a common course of things, ought to yield to the extraordinary nature of the crisis.

What Governor Jay thought of this we do not know. He did not answer it. He wrote on the back, "Proposing a measure for party purposes which it would not become me to adopt," and stuck it into a remote pigeonhole of his desk, where it was discovered many years later, after his death, and published.

★ 19 ★

A Day of Mud and Dirty Snow

★ The Grand Columbian Federal City was rising, lumpily, amid clouds of dust, splatterings of mud, and the buzz of 10 million mosquitoes. It was now being called Washington, and it presented a dreary prospect. Atop its highest hill, which overlooked the Potomac, two bright white buildings shone. Between them was an empty space. One building was the Senate house, already occupied by that august body, for it was almost completed. The other building, by no means finished, though it had been roofed, was meant to contain the House of Representatives, presently cramped into a dim corner of the Senatorial edifice. The gap between these structures according to plans would one day be filled by a home for the Supreme Court, which would be capped by an enormous dome.

On the slopes of this Capitol Hill-to-be were sundry wooden buildings, most no more than shacks. Seven or eight of them were boardinghouses, all filled to capacity. No hotels had yet been built in the city. There were a tailor shop, a shoemaker's, a printer's, a grocery, a pamphlet-and-stationery store, a dry-goods store, and an oyster house.

The most pretentious boardinghouse was on the south side of the hill, at about what is now New Jersey Avenue and C Street. It was Conrad and McMunn's boardinghouse, a huge place, a veritable cowstable. Jefferson lived there, and so did Gallatin, and twenty-five to thirty others, including two women, and they all ate at a common table. Jefferson, who after all was the Vice President of the United States, had a bedroom to himself and from time to time the use of a downstairs sitting room, but Gallatin had to share his sleeping quarters with another Congressman. Each paid fifteen dollars a week, which included three meals a day, wine, service, and firewood. Gallatin thought it was too much, considering the food. The beef wasn't very good, he said, and there were seldom any vegetables. Jefferson made no complaint.

Stretching westward from this hill for a little over a mile was a thoroughfare the sides of which were roughly defined by sticks thrust into the earth, though for the most part, like the surrounding territory, it consisted of alder bushes, mud holes, horse apples, tree stumps, and tangles of wild grapevine. This "road" was the rather grandly named Pennsylvania Avenue. At its far end was the White House, more often called the President's palace, on which workingmen were still working. There were no lawn, no fence, no garden.

The house was officially known as the Executive Mansion, and there had been a contest for the best plan for it, a contest which Thomas Jefferson had entered—anonymously of course. The Vice President's proposal had called for a porticoed dome design based on Palladio's Villa Rotunda near Vicenza, a house Jefferson had in fact never seen, though he had studied the plans, for he was a great admirer of Palladio. This proposal had been turned down.

Still farther west, in the Potomac Hills, was Georgetown, where twenty-odd houses had been built, some of brick, all of them handsome, but this was a separate community, not part of Washington, D.C.

The city itself was set in a swamp and seethed with mosquitoes.

It was even hard to *find*. John Adams went there in June, to open the new session of Congress, and he put up in a boardinghouse, while Abigail, back in Braintree, worried about him. It was November before the second First Lady thought that she was well enough to make the trip, and then, somewhere south of Baltimore, she and her party actually got lost in the woods. They threshed about for two hours, unable to find again the trail they had somehow mislaid. Finally, a Negro slave, gathering firewood for his master, came upon them and guided them to the proper path.

When Abigail did reach Washington, she must have wished that she hadn't. The White House was a disgrace. November was very wet and cold that year, and the plaster in the walls had not dried, making the mansion dank. Abigail reckoned that they would have to keep fires in all thirteen of the fireplaces in order to live in the place, and with the price of wood what it was in Washington—like the price of everything else—she really wondered whether they could afford that, on John's salary.

Meanwhile, the campaign continued. There were no crowds, no spread-eagle oratory, no parades. The newspapers on both sides raged sulfurously, but they had always done that. There were no torches, no red fires, no bands or banners. President Adams did make a few speeches here and there, in the new capital before it was officially opened, and also on the way to and from Braintree, but that was his custom anyway. Thomas Jefferson said nothing publicly.

It might have been supposed—and many historians have supposed it—that the Alien and Sedition Acts, a direct threat to American freedom, an insult to the American people, would greatly affect the election. They did not. Democratic Congressmen were outraged and even moderate Federalists like John Marshall were troubled by these enactments, and if ever the War Whoopers had got their way, the Acts would indeed have been dangerous. The War Whoopers, however, did not. One of the Acts, the Enemy Alien Act, a wartime measure, never did go into effect.

The others were temporary measures and would soon be doomed if the Republicans prevailed in the forthcoming election or perhaps even if they didn't. They were enforced spottily and without much effect, and the victims, all of course Republican-Democrats, did not suffer greatly.

The Alien and Sedition Acts, which loomed so large in the minds of indignant recorders of these events, played little part if they played any at all in the Presidential campaign of 1800. The issues, rather, were personal, even though the newspapers still screamed. A few editors were tossed into jail by Federalist judges, but that did not bring any pause in the hurling of verbal barbs, and there were few *new* charges.

Thomas Jefferson was no longer pelted with the epithet "coward" because as wartime governor of Virginia he had eluded arrest by the British soldiery, but to offset this moderation the "atheism" accusation was redoubled. Solemn ministers, especially in the Congregational meetinghouses, solemnly assured their congregations that a Republican victory would bring the slavering Frenchmen in droves to these angelic shores, and the women were warned that they should not depend upon the Bible for solace when they were penned in military brothels, for unless they hid the Bibles very carefully, these books would be seized and publicly burned.

One fresh snippet of scandal did make its appearance, though somewhat belatedly. This was a letter Jefferson had written to Philip Mazzei, who for a while had been his neighbor in Virginia but who had returned to his native Italy. In it the Vice President referred to "men who were Samsons in the field and Solomons in the council, but who have had their heads shorn by the harlot England."

Jefferson had thought that the letter was a private communication, but Mazzei, delighted, turned it over to a Florentine journal, which published it—in Italian. This was picked up by the Paris *Moniteur* and translated into French. The next to see it, months afterward, was the lexicographer Noah Webster, an ardent Federalist and the publisher of the New York *Minerva*. Webster had rendered it back into English again—it is notable that his version differed little from the original, despite all the translations—and published it in the *Minerva*. It had made a great splash, and the Federalists reprinted it again and again in their pamphlets, pointing out that one of those who were "Samsons in the field," etc., undoubtedly was meant to be George Washington, who was still alive at that time, though no longer President. The idea, of course, had been to make Jefferson look like an enemy of the Father of his Country. Neither man ever made any public statement on the matter.

Now the Federalists had revived the so-called Mazzei letter with a beating of drums and a tootling of horns, in the hope that it would increase their chances of being called the Washington party. It is to be doubted that it made any difference in the election, one way or the other.

As for the denigration of John Adams, the Republican editors, though they labored mightily, could have saved themselves that trouble. The work was being done for them by a Federalist. As early as May 10 Alexander Hamilton had put himself on record as preferring even Thomas Jefferson to John Adams. "If we must have an enemy at the head of the government," he wrote to Theodore Sedgwick, "let it be one whom we can oppose, and for whom we will not be responsible, who will not involve our party in the disgrace of his foolish and bad measures."

However, all was not lost. Hamilton still favored the "sneak" election of Charles Cotesworth Pinckney, "the only thing that can possibly save us from the fangs of Jefferson." Just the same, on August 1, he addressed himself directly to the President, at the same time seeing that the press got a copy of the letter, and angrily asked Mr. Adams if he had indeed "asserted the existence of a British faction in this country" to which he, Hamilton, might be said to belong.

No other conclusion can be drawn from this letter than that Hamilton was up to his old tricks: he was looking for a fight. He may have hoped to provoke an indiscreet reply that would be useful to him in his anti-Adams campaign. But no matter how far gone he might be in the madness induced by desperation, he could hardly have expected that this letter would be taken seriously by John Adams, whose religious convictions would have caused him to shy in horror from the duello, even if his common sense did not.

Adams, of course, did not answer. Hamilton let a month go by, and then wrote again, asserting "that by whomsoever a charge of the kind mentioned in my former letter, may, at any time, have been made or insinuated against me, it is a base, wicked, and cruel calumny; destitute even of a plausible pretext, to excuse the folly, or mask the depravity which must have dictated it."

It is hard to see what the ex-Secretary of the Treasury had in mind here. Perhaps he was launching the yet unformed American dueling convention of "posting" a man, who wouldn't acknowledge your challenge, by publicly calling him harsh names such as "cow-hearted poltroon," "liverbellied rascal," and the like.

"Posting" was to be confined to the Southern part of the United States, though even there it was never quite respectable, and it was unknown in Alexander Hamilton's day.

It is even harder to see what Hamilton had in mind when next he took up his pen. Waxing vitriolic over and beyond the call of political duty, he wrote a pamphlet, a paper, something, that was entitled "The Public Conduct and Character of John Adams, Esq., President of the United States." Some of the material for this eruption of muck he had got from Timothy Pickering, who at his request stole bits of the President's boyhood diary from the national archives as he was cleaning out his desk at State. Other snippets came from Oliver Wolcott, who was still in the Cabinet, though working through friends for a Pinckney victory. None of it was damning, and much made no sense. The ex-Secretary did rail against the President for opposing his bid for the inspector generalship of the army, but otherwise he set forth no *specific* objections to John Adams either as a man or a party leader. He only wrote of Adams' "great and intrinsic defects in character, which unfit him for the office of chief magistrate" and his "disgusting egotism, distempered jealousy, and ungovernable indiscretion."

Hamilton meant this paper not for general consumption—it might be misunderstood—but only for the eyes of men whom he was wont to designate as "those of the first class," in other words, the really *high* High Federalists. Still, there were so many such men that he thought he ought to have the "Public Conduct and Character" in a form more convenient for distribution. Therefore, he sent it to a printer.

Aaron Burr, who knew everybody, knew that printer. Even before Hamilton got his own copies, the "Conduct and Character" was appearing, in full, in the Philadelphia *Aurora* and the New London *Bee*. The editors of these Republican journals were under indictment for violation of the Sedition Act, but that did not keep them from publishing such a glorious sewer of spite.

Bit by bit the news of the several state elections drifted in. It was going to be a very close contest.

Burr was wrong about Rhode Island, which stuck to its Federalist heritage. *All* of New England remained Federalist.

New Jersey's 7 electoral votes and Delaware's 3 were Federalist, but Maryland split it right down the middle—5 for each. North Carolina too turned in a split vote: 8 for Jefferson—Burr, 4 for Adams—Pinckney. The holdout Federalists of Pennsylvania continued to threaten to negate that state's delegation, until at last the Republicans, though a large majority, agreed to a split: 8 for them, 7 for the Federalists.

Virginia had the unit-rule system, and all 19 of her votes went Republican-Democrat.

Georgia, with 4 electoral votes, was firmly Republican. It would take some time for the states on the other side of the mountains to get their results to the capital city, but they both operated under the unit rule and were safely Republican, so it was known that the result would be: Kentucky 4, Tennessee 3.

That made it 65 to 65 coming to the last state to elect electors, South Carolina.

Just what happened in South Carolina we do not know. South Carolina elected its electors by means of its legislature, and the legislators were a clubby lot, many of them kin to each other. It seems that the friends of Charles Cotesworth Pinckney, inspired by the machinations of the former Secretary of the Treasury, believed for a little while that they could get their man in—

as President, that is, not merely as Vice President. But when Pinckney himself learned of this he said no. He was a gentleman, and he would have no part of any such political hanky-panky.

Charles (no middle name) Pinckney, a young United States Senator, first cousin to John Adams' running mate, and the "black sheep" of his family because he had turned Republican, had another explanation for the 1800 result in South Carolina. He said that the Hamilton conspirators had virtually had the thing sewed up when he himself came charging in to rally the true Republican-Democrats and to scatter the Hamiltonians by showing them "The Public Conduct and Character of John Adams, Esq., President of the United States," and asking them if *that* was the kind of man they meant to sell their souls for.

Whichever Pinckney story was true—and they could both have been—the Republicans of South Carolina, in a sensational last-minute flipflop, triumphed. All 8 of the state's electoral votes went to Jefferson–Burr.

It was a cold, dark day, a day of mud and dirty snow, February 11, 1801, when at last Thomas Jefferson, as Vice President, presided over a joint session of Congress, and read the official result: Jefferson 73, Burr 73, Adams 65, C. C. Pinckney 64, John Jay 1.

Somebody in New England, in Rhode Island, some anonymous elector, had cast his second vote for Jay, presumably in order to avoid an Adams–Pinckney tie.

★ 20 ★

Hail to the Chief!

★ The Republican-Democrats had won. Nobody questioned that. There was a great deal of doubt, however, about who would be the next President of the United States, assuming that there *would* be one.

After the Vice President's announcement the House of Representatives retired to its dim temporary quarters. Here was the body upon which the fate of the country now hung. The Constitution had provided only that each elector should vote for two men, and that the man who got the largest number of votes would become President, while the one who got the second-largest number of votes would become Vice President. In the event of a tie, the Constitution stipulated, the House of Representatives should decide between the two.

The House, however, was now a lame-duck body. The new Senate was to be divided exactly in half, which meant that with the Vice President's deciding vote in the case of a tie it would be Republican. The incoming House, to take its seat on March 4 at the same time as the new President—whoever he might be— would consist of sixty-six Republicans and forty Federalists. Yet it was the lame-duck House that had to decide this matter, and *it* was, though ever so slightly, Federalist.

The vote, moreover, must be by states, each state counting as a unit, and an absolute majority of all the states would be required for a choice. Since there were sixteen states, that meant nine.

The hall was chilly. Something had gone wrong with the heating. As they sat there in the cold, here is the way the Representatives voted that first day, February 11, and it was a pattern that was to continue:

	Jefferson	Burr
New Hampshire	0	6
Vermont	1	1
Massachusetts	3	11
Rhode Island	0	2
Connecticut	0	7
New York	6	4
New Jersey	3	2
Pennsylvania	9	4
Delaware	0	1
Maryland	4	4
Virginia	14	5
North Carolina	6	4
South Carolina	1	4
Georgia	1	0
Kentucky	2	0
Tennessee	1	0
TOTALS	51	55

The number of electors alloted to each state was, of course, equivalent to the combined number of United States Senators and members of the House of Representatives that the state had. Therefore, the vote in the House for each state was two fewer—the two Senators—than the electoral vote for that state.

The states might split their vote, as many did, but the winner must get the majority of *states,* rather than the majority of *votes.*

Burr, as can be seen above, had 55 votes, Jefferson only 51, but eight of the states favored Jefferson—New York, New Jersey, Pennsylvania, Virginia, North Carolina, Kentucky, Georgia, and Tennessee—while only six—New Hampshire, Massachusetts, Connecticut, Delaware, Rhode Island, and South Carolina— plumped for Aaron Burr. Two states, Maryland and Vermont, split their votes evenly, 4 to 4 and 1 to 1, so they were not counted.

Jefferson needed to get only one more state. *One* vote, properly placed—for instance, in Vermont, Maryland, or Delaware—would do it for him.

On the other hand, Burr, though he had the larger number of individual votes, would have needed the diversion of 1 each in three states—Vermont, Maryland, and New Jersey.

What had happened, of course, was that the Federalists, knocked back on their heels by a Republican victory, had rallied to the realization that even though the next President might be one of those despised creatures, the world would not necessarily come to an end. The Federalists controlled the lame-duck Congress.

It was, indeed, a happy position for the Federalists. All they needed to do was go to the two Republican contenders—very quietly, of course, leaving no record of the interviews—and, playing them off one against the other, make a deal.

The Federalists, "the wise, the rich, and the well-born," were cynical men. They assumed that anybody in public life, and certainly any *Democrat,* would sell out his supporters if the price was right.

Certainly they tried, and they tried very hard. They simply could not believe it, the way their offers were turned down.

The House of Representatives in its drafty quarters took a second vote. It came out exactly the same: eight states for Jefferson, six states for Burr—the same eight, the same six.

The House prepared to vote again. The weather worsened.

Who would be the third President of the United States?

There were five more ballots, quickly. The Representatives sent out for food and drink. They stayed up all night, not arguing, not orating, just casting their votes. There was no change. The last was the same as the first had been.

Why did not President Adams do something about this impasse? We do not know. He has told us a great deal about his acts and his aspirations, his thoughts and even his dreams, as President of the United States, for he had always been garrulous and in his old age he was to wax more worried than ever about posterity, but he did not explain his silence during the Jefferson–Burr poll. Apparently the election had been a shock to him, for he had not expected to lose. Anyway, now he had papers to sign.

Late in December, sensing what was about to happen, Congress had taken steps to ensure that the nation's judgeships should remain in the hands of the Federalist party. The Judiciary Act created six new federal circuit courts, with *sixteen* new judges, all to be appointed for life. It also created various minor posts the new District of Columbia, and one provision of it stipulated that when the next Supreme Court vacancy occurred it should not be filled, thus cutting the court from six justices to five. The reason for this last, seemingly strange provision was given as the need to avert a tie vote, but everyone knew that the real reason was to keep the Republican-Democrats from getting a seat on the Supreme Court bench.

The appointment of marshals, collectors, justices of the peace, district attorneys, besides the new judges themselves, called for a great deal of signing, and applications were pouring in from all over the country.

So Adams signed papers while the House of Representatives wearily renewed its voting. A member from Maryland, a Jeffersonian, Joseph Nicholson, who was suffering from pneumonia and would have risked his life by going outdoors in that weather, had his friends bring a cot for him, and he remained right there. He knew that if he missed a single ballot the whole state of Maryland would go for Burr, which might be the first tumbling stone in an avalanche.

What about Burr himself? And what about Thomas Jefferson?

The arch-schemer, the hero of the Manhattan Company coup, had himself been sent to the New York State legislature in that historic election last spring, and he believed that his duties should keep him in Albany. Also, his beloved daughter Theodosia, his only child—the only *legitimate* one, anyway—was about to get married, there in Albany, to a rich young Southern planter, Joseph Alston. The proud papa could hardly be expected to bother with a Presidential election when he had such a momentous matter on his hands.

The wedding ceremony took place on February 2, but even after that Aaron Burr did not go to the raw little town of Washington. He had stated in letters to friends—letters he had given those friends permission to publish—that he considered himself a Vice Presidential candidate and that in the event of a tie he would of course take second place to his friend the party leader, Thomas Jefferson. Assumedly he said the same thing to the various Federalist agents who sought him out at Albany, whispering offers. At least one of those agents, young David A. Ogden of New York City, who had recently become a law partner of Alexander Hamilton, returned from Albany cursing the man because he would not listen to reason, would not promise to leave the Hamilton national banking system and the United States Navy untouched, and would not promise to abstain from firing minor federal officials, even to become President. It was, Ogden thought, downright unpatriotic. He was disgusted.

All through that wet, cold week, while the capital teemed with rumors of armed bands of frontiersmen about to come storming out of the West and with tales of militiamen in each of the states poised for a descent upon Washington, the House of Representatives went on doggedly taking ballots—with no change.

The Senate too, in its grander quarters, met every day, but the Senate had nothing to do; everything depended upon the House.

What would happen if no decision was reached by March 4?

Would John Adams continue to be President? Or could he appoint his own successor, on a temporary basis? Or could he or Congress decree another national election? Or—what?

Perhaps those wild frontiersmen would come over the horizon after all, with their long Kentucky rifles, their long knives. Thousands believed that they would. Men were hiding valuables, barricading doors.

"Since it was evidently the intention of our fellow citizens to make Mr. Jefferson their President, it seems proper to fulfil that intention." There spoke common sense, in the person of Gouverneur Morris, late ambassador to France. Another High Federalist, Theodore Sedgwick, agreed with him, but these men stood alone. Besides, since they were Senators, they had nothing to say in the poll that was being taken.

The nineteenth ballot showed no shift, as did the twentieth . . . the twenty-first. . . .

The Federalists could have closed this contest at any time if they had only got together and agreed upon backing Burr, as most of them in fact did, in the belief that Burr would be an easier man to make a deal with. But the party was hopelessly split between the High Federalists and the rank and file, sometimes called the Half-Federalists, between the Hamiltonians and the Adamsites. Some stubbornly clung to the belief that, really, the American people had chosen Jefferson as President, and that Jefferson therefore should be declared to have been elected. Others favored a scheme by which the president of the Senate, a Federalist, by act of Congress should be proclaimed the temporary emergency President of the United States until another national election could be held. Or perhaps this should be done with the Speaker of the House, who also was a Federalist.

Hamilton himself? His stand varied. At one time he was sure that *anything* would be justified that might serve to keep the country "from the fangs of Jefferson," but a little later he was to aver that even Jefferson would be better than more of John Adams. After his plans for C. C. Pinckney collapsed, he appeared to favor Jefferson, at least as opposed to Aaron Burr. "Jefferson," he wrote, "is by far not so dangerous a man; and he has pretensions to character." Yet for a while he might have toyed with the idea of playing the two against one another in the hope of getting a Federalist President after all, if only temporarily. He certainly knew of Ogden's trip to Albany. But at last he pronounced Burr unacceptable, and that was to be his final word.

Some historians have stated—and indeed, the temptation to do so is hard to resist—that Thomas Jefferson owed his election as President of the United States to his bitterest enemy, Alexander Hamilton. This is oversimplication; it overlooks the fact that in 1801 Hamilton was no longer the dauntless leader of the government party but a discredited politician.

On the morning of Friday, February 14, the thirty-first, thirty-second, and thirty-third ballots were taken, and there was no change. Then Representative James A. Bayard of Delaware proposed that the House adjourn until Monday morning. Everybody knew that this presaged a deal.

The Vice President, after presiding at the stiff, short, formal sessions of the Senate each morning, had been holding a series of small conferences in the downstairs parlor that the proprietors of his boardinghouse had turned over to him. No word ever came out of those conferences—to this day none has—but it was known that Bayard, himself a Federalist, had either attended a few or been represented at them. The smallest state in population, Delaware had only one Representative in the House, and Bayard, until this time, had consistently voted for Burr. If he went to Jefferson, it would be the whole state going to Jefferson, making the needed ninth.

On Monday morning, on the thirty-sixth ballot, that is exactly what happened. Jefferson was elected. The nation could breathe again.

On the night of March 3, the night before the inauguration, John Adams stayed up late—for him. It was nine o'clock before he finished signing all those commissions, appointments, warrants. He was up at dawn, to supervise the last-minute packing. He had ordered a coach around, early though it was. He was *damned* if he would go to the inauguration with that man Jefferson. Un-hailed, indeed unnoticed, he rode north out of town.

Already the sky was clearing. It would be a fine day, after all that bad weather.

The cannons began to boom, announcing the inauguration of the third President of the United States, who soon would be saying to the crowd: "Every difference of opinion is not a difference of principle. We have called by different names brethren of the same principle. We are all Republicans, we are all Federalists."

But John Adams did not hear that, for he was too far away. He was going back to Braintree.

★ 21 ★

No Time to Falter

★ It has been called the Second American Revolution, but it was not a revolution. The skies did not fall. No tidal wave engulfed the land. Though a believer in religious freedom had been elected President, the government still functioned. Nobody went bankrupt. And after a long while, timorously, breath well bated, the little old ladies of Connecticut crept out of their cellars to learn that the meetinghouse had not been burned by slavering atheistic French soldiers, that they themselves would not be hurled into brothels, and that they might keep their Bibles as long as they pleased. It was all a bit heady, being so unexpected.

The banks too remained unrazed. The new Chief Executive, it turned out, did not hate and fear *all* banks, only those that were run on public funds for the benefit of full-time professional speculators. He even produced a banking genius of his own, Albert Gallatin, the originator of the House Ways and Means Committee, who was now made Secretary of the Treasury. Largely it would seem because he had a German accent, Gallatin, a Swiss aristocrat by birth, was hated by the Federalists, and he cemented that hatred into place when he began to juggle figures with a brilliancy and speed that made Alexander Hamilton look like a bungler. For this the Federalists never forgave him.

It might be supposed then that when half a continent was offered, at a next-to-nothing price, Thomas Jefferson would not falter. But he did.

Robert Livingston, the ambassador to France, was a Federalist, but the President had sent James Monroe, a Republican, to assist him. These two had orders to buy the city of New Orleans and if necessary a small chunk of West Florida as well. In any event, they were authorized to go as high as $10 million for control of the mouth of the Mississippi River.

France, since she began to kick up her political heels, had been many things as power moved from Girondists to Jacobins to the Committee of Public Safety to the Directory. Power was now lodged in a consulate of three, even though nobody could remember who the second and third consuls were, so emphatically had the first, the swarthy little general from Corsica, taken over. Napoleon Bonaparte *was* France. *L'état, c'était lui.* When he broke in upon the negotiations that his minister Prince Talleyrand was properly and polysyllabically conducting with Livingston and Monroe, it was to suggest that the visitors buy not only the city of New Orleans but the whole territory of Louisiana. He further suggested that they do this right away. He was not a man who liked to be kept waiting.

Hastily Talleyrand and his assistant, Barbé-Marbois, consulted. They came up with the price of 80 million French francs, of which 60 million should be cash down.

The ambassadors agreed. This would be the biggest real estate deal in history.

But it had not been finalized! The rest was up to Thomas Jefferson, who could repudiate the action—after all, the ambassadors had not been authorized to make any such arrangement—by simply refusing to give the treaty to the Senate.

Jefferson hesitated.

Nobody knew, really, how large Louisiana was. It was certainly almost four times the size of the original thirteen colonies, about three times the size of Italy, more than seven times the size of Great Britain and Ireland combined. Its acquisition would double the United States territorially.

Eighty million francs would amount to about $15 million. By calling Louisiana 1 million square miles (a fair guess at the time—actually, it was to prove to be 875,025 square miles), it came out to about four cents a square mile.

The government did not have anything like $15 million to spare, but it was not this fact that gave Jefferson pause. He disagreed with the notion that a public debt was a public blessing, and from the time of his inauguration he had been working to pay off the obligations his administration had inherited.

But a mere matter of $15 million wouldn't have deterred him.

He was worried, for one thing, about the Indians. Nobody knew much about Louisiana, really, and it was certain that nobody had the slightest idea of how many Indians lived there. Suppose they numbered millions? What would happen to them? Already many of the men who were settling the West were clamoring for permission to push the scattered, scared Indians across the Mississippi. What would happen if that land, too, became United States territory?

He worried even more about his constitutional rights. He had been preaching strict construction; it was, he used to declare, "the very breath of my political life." Yet where in the Constitution did it say that the national government could acquire, by purchase or otherwise, outside land? The Federalists, by overstraining the theory of implied powers, might pretend to find some such permission, but Mr. Jefferson could not.

The Federalists, in fact, were doing exactly what an opposition party naturally would do, what a little while ago they would have branded as treasonous or at best in very bad taste: They were opposing a government policy only because they feared that its fulfillment might strengthen the government. Their controlled press cried that $15 million was too high a price. They were pointing out that Manhattan had been bought for trade goods worth about $24; that Ferdinando Gorges had sold the whole province of Maine for £1,250; that William Penn had paid only a few thousand pounds for Pennsylvania. Why, $15 million, these desperate men cried, represented three dollars for every man, woman, and child in the country!

This clamor did not faze the President, who had enough to think about. Though Livingston and Monroe were writing from Paris begging him to act lest the temperamental French dictator change his mind, Jefferson started to frame a Constitutional amendment that would give the President the right to buy Louisiana—or almost anything else. He had called a special session of Congress.

He did not like what he had wrought, however, and neither did his consultants and advisers. He scrapped it and wrote another, but this one too, the advisers agreed, sounded "sacred." It wouldn't do. He scrapped *it*.

Others were tinkering with the same thought. The second President's glowering son, an undiplomatic diplomat, John Quincy Adams, concocted what he hoped would prove to be a model amendment making the Purchase possible. However, it proved to be full of legal loopholes and was discarded. The Secretary of State, the Father of the Constitution, James Madison, framed one that was simple and admirably short: "Louisiana is hereby admitted to this Union." Nobody paid attention to it.

Friends urged upon the President that the treaty-making power conferred by the Constitution would cover the Louisiana Purchase, making an amendment unnecessary. But "If the treaty-making power is boundless, then we have no Constitution," he wailed.

Delay could be fatal. The bargain was too good to be turned down. Sighing sadly, Thomas Jefferson accepted the doctrine of implied powers long enough to submit the treaty to the United States Senate, whilst the Federalists screamed.

Thus, it was a double flipflop. Each side exactly reversed itself, and the timing was perfect.

It took more than a week for Congress to get a quorum, and

then, after less than four days of debate, the Senate ratified the treaty 24–7.

Here the House tried to get into the act, as it had done at the time of the Jay treaty of 1796. A Federalist representative from New York, Gaylord Griswold, introduced a resolution calling for a better look at the French claim to Louisiana. *Did* France in fact have a right to dispose of the place, seeing that Bonaparte had promised never to sell or cede it? The vote was close—59 to 57— but Griswold's resolution lost. Jefferson, a doubting Thomas, had triumphed.

The few Federalists who were left, mostly in New England, like the Old Guard were prepared to die but never surrender. There was talk of secession, and they might have tried this had they been able to get a President from New York who could bring that needed state along with him. Both Aaron Burr and Alexander Hamilton were considered. Burr happened to be Vice President of the United States, but it was assumed that he would switch sides in an instant if he was offered the top post. Yet the man either was true to his oath of office—a possibility that did not seem to have occurred to the New Englanders—or else he was too smart to lend his name to such doings. As for Hamilton, he no longer counted politically. When Washington died, so had Hamilton's standing as a statesman. He was shrill, he was colorful, but his prestige was gone. He was a faded man.

Hamilton himself did not agree with this estimate. A natural fighter, a gamecock, he did not propose to sit still and watch the political party he had created vanish like so much steam. He might yet look upon the public as "a great *beast,* sir!" but he could at last perceive the need for feeding this beast. He sat down and wrote a plan for the reorganization of the Federalist party along almost democratic lines. He might have winced while he did this; but he did it.

The Christian Constitutional Society, as he now called it, would employ "all lawful means in *concert* to promote the election of

fit men." It should be administered by a national Federalist council to consist of a president and twelve members, of whom four
and the president would constitute a quorum, and under this by
"sub-directing councils" in each state. These should strive for
"the cultivation of popular favor by fair and justifiable exped-
ients"; they should pay much more attention to immigrants and
workingmen; and they should make themselves heard by the
students in the schools.

Rexford Tugwell and Joseph Dorfman, contemporary historians,
have called this proposal "the lowest Hamilton ever fell" but it
seems to others the highest that he ever reached. However, it
came too late. The party of "the wise, the well-born, and the
rich" had gone too far along the path of self-righteousness to be
halted by a command to regard the American people.

Besides, Hamilton was a failure. He had lost. His conversion
policy had resulted in malodorous scandals. His protective tariff
and his direct taxes were being dropped, without ill effect to the
economy. The national bank, his pride and joy, was proving unpopular and in places downright inefficient, and when its franchise ran out in a few years, it would almost certainly be dis-
continued. His federal debt was being whittled away by those
damned Republican rascals in Washington, who, refusing to be
daunted by the threat of a military takeover, had reduced the
army's appropriation.

Even the great Hamilton showpiece, Paterson, New Jersey,
was on the rocks. S.U.M. stood for Society for Useful Manufactures. Hamilton had designed it from top to bottom, naming it
after his partner, William Paterson, ex-Congressman, former Attorney General, former governor, presently a justice of the Supreme Court. S.U.M. had been granted a charter under which it,
a private corporation, was given exclusive jurisdiction over thirty-
six square miles of property at the head of navigation of the
Passaic River, where it could exercise eminent domain, where it
was free of all taxation, and where its employees were to be
forever exempt from personal taxation and militia duty. Even so,

it had failed. Hamilton could no longer keep it alive by pumping money into it, for he had no more money to pump. He had lost a fortune speculating in land he'd never seen in western New York State, and he was deeply in debt.

So—why listen to Hamilton? One by one the New England nabobs turned down, in a chilly silence, the Christian Constitutional Society plan.

"Aaron Burr's pistol blew the brains out of the Federalist party," it was fashionable to say at one time. But the statement was incorrect. The pistol was not Burr's; he had never owned one. The pistols, both of them, belonged to Hamilton's brother-in-law, John Barker Church. Hamilton, through his representative, had won the privilege of providing the weapons. He had also won the toss for picking the site of the fight and for speaking the signal to fire. Hamilton indeed was given every possible break in the arrangements.

He had been insulting Burr for years in private company, declaring again and again that the man was a liar, but not until he put his opinion into print—at second hand, by means of a meddlesome minister—could he be challenged. That was the way the code worked in New York at the time. Burr sent the clipping to Hamilton, and he demanded, stiffly but politely enough, an explanation. The ex-Secretary, a prodigious letter writer, ordinarily was direct, forthright, crisp, but in the ensuing correspondence with Burr he became evasive, flopping about like a fish that tries to shake itself off the hook. Representatives were appointed—friends, respectable men who would see that everything was done right. Hamilton was given every chance to apologize or at least explain, but this he refused to do. Eventually Burr called him out.

Then these two short men, these discredited middle-aged politicians, took position in a glade in Weehawken of a bright, cheerful morning, Wednesday, July 11, 1804, and shot at one another.

Hamilton's bullet went through a cedar at a point about 12½ feet above the ground and 4 feet off the line of fire, to his right.

Burr's bullet went into Hamilton's belly near the middle, clipped a false rib, smashed both liver and diaphragm, and lodged in the second lumbar vertebra.

Hamilton lived in great pain for about thirty-one hours, and when he died, he was canonized. This would have amazed the man himself. For all his pretensions he had never aspired to sainthood.

Pistol duels were almost as common in the New York area then as in Charleston or New Orleans, and they excited as little talk. Yet the din after the Weehawken affair was deafening. Preachers thundered, orators denounced, societies passed condemnatory resolutions, and the growling of the crowds in the street grew so loud that Aaron Burr thought it best to slip away to Philadelphia, where friends, the Biddles, put him up.

Meanwhile, a coroner's jury in New York had found him guilty of murder, though the deed had been done in New Jersey. In fact, a grand jury of Bergen County, New Jersey, where there was no law against dueling, had indicted him.

The hullabaloo continued and even swelled, when it was learned that Hamilton had left a statement, written some time before the duel, in which he protested that he bore no ill will against Colonel Burr, said that he was sorry to be hurting his wife and children and also his many creditors, and insisted that he had always discountenanced dueling. "My religious and moral principles are strongly opposed to the practice of Duelling and it would ever give me pain to be obliged to shed the blood of a fellow creature in a private combat forbidden by the laws." These curious remarks might have gone unnoticed if the Livingstons and the Clintons had not seized upon them as evidence that Burr had fired early, before the signal, and that Hamilton had deliberately delayed his shot.

There was not a grain of truth in this story, or in the assertions of the Clintons and Livingstons and their friends high and low that Colonel Burr was a crack shot who had practiced every day before the duel. Here was a heaven-sent opportunity to "get"

Burr by making him into a devil, while at the same time trans-
forming Hamilton, whom they had hated, into a saint. Burr was
getting too big for his breeches. He must be so bedaubed with
obloquy that he would never dare to come home.

Only two men saw the duel: William P. Van Ness for Burr,
Nathaniel Pendleton for Hamilton. The surgeon, Dr. David Hosack,
had just left the boat that brought him, and was scrambling up a
path between bushes, when the shots rang out.

Van Ness said that both fired at the same instant. Judge
Pendleton agreed, but he believed that his principal had meant
to throw away his shot and had pulled the trigger only as he had
been hit—a spasmodic act, an involuntary act.

At ten paces there was never any question of *marksmanship*.
A blind man couldn't have missed. It was entirely a matter of
speed, and Burr's hand, it must be assumed, was the quicker.

The Republican machine men fell upon the Pendleton story,
shouting again and again that General Hamilton had held back
and had been slain in cold blood by Colonel Burr, who knew
this. They did not explain why Hamilton had not fired straight
up, as was the custom under these conditions, but dangerously low
and to his right, the side on which the seconds stood. A man who
meant to throw his fire away would not do that. It wasn't that he
did not know where the seconds were. Just before the signal he
had begged for yet another delay, a very brief one, and from
beneath his coat he had fished a pair of spectacles (he never
wore them in public) which he carefully put on before nodding
a go-ahead.

In ordinary circumstances there would have been nothing remarkable here. But the circumstances were not ordinary. Burr
was a dangerous man, and he made an ideal villain, with his
bland, sleepy smile and his refusal to deny anything. Bucket after
bucket of tar was poured upon him and upon the memory of
him. And thus it was that he was sent to hell, his adversary at the
same time, though only as a side-result, being sent to Heaven.
Wrote Herbert Agar in *Price of Union:*

As clearly as any Northern soldier in the Civil War, Hamilton fought for the Union. He believed that if he refused the duel his own political influence would be destroyed, and that at some future date Burr might break the nation. He believed that if he accepted the duel but refused to fire, and if Burr then killed him, Burr would ruin himself as well. So he went to Weehawken, and threw away his fire, and died from Burr's first bullet.

★ 22 ★

Who Won?

★ A great turn had been made, a new course was being pursued. Could Jefferson survive? Thanks to Louisiana, he prospered.

The Federalist party, unabashed by anyone's bullet, knocked itself out. Staggering wildly, lurching like a drunkard, it kept going, somehow, until the Presidential election of 1816, when the Federalist candidate Rufus King lost to James Monroe 183 to 34. Then the party simply dissolved, and not many sighs were wafted after it.

The United States had become a one-party nation, but already that party was splitting itself down the center.

Who, then, won? If either Jefferson or Hamilton triumphed, which was it? The outcome of the confrontation at Weehawken is known: The "winner" there lost, the "loser" won. But what of the much more important duel when Thomas Jefferson and Alexander Hamilton faced one another, over the years, "like pitted cocks"? How did that contest end, or could it be said to *have* ended, even now?

To put it another way: Did either man come to see, or would he see if he were alive today, his patriotic heart's desire?

Thomas Jefferson is popularly pictured as a dreamer who hated cities with all their dirt and stink, favoring a countryside filled with pirouetting peasants and with shepherdesses who sang of the joys of the soil. Yet he was a practical politician, a master organizer, a relentless follower-up, known, when he was Secretary of State, for his tough line of dealing. Once, on a memorable occasion, when Vice President, he had toasted "Eternal union of sentiments between the commerce and agriculture of our country." He meant it too. He no more thought that all farmers were honest and all traders thieves than Alexander Hamilton believed the opposite, but he *preferred* the farmers.

Jefferson believed that a corporation was a thing economically repugnant and constitutionally illicit. To Hamilton a corporation was a useful expression of governmental authority; he was a corporate man. Today the United States is corporation-ridden. What a few private businesses there might be left are being sluiced toward the gaping maw of conglomeration. The national government is more powerful than ever, the states proportionately weaker.

Jefferson believed that government should be "a few plain duties to be performed by a few servants." The United States today supports a bureaucracy bigger than any other known to history.

"The ideal of Hamilton was the hive, the ideal of Jefferson was the bee," wrote historian Frederick Scott Oliver. Jefferson was for the small man, the artisan. Hamilton was for the wealthy one, the man who managed others.

Hamilton was concerned with property rights, not human rights, which were Jefferson's field. Hamilton believed that the richer the rich become, the better it is for the poor. He believed that if you poured money over the top of the pile some of it, eventually, might work its way down to those who were near the bottom. It seemed to him the natural way of running things. This trickle-down theory has its supporters even today, perhaps more of them than ever.

Hamilton believed that a millionaire could do no wrong, a notion even more widespread today than it was in his time. Jefferson believed that the countinghouse had a place in American life, yes, but that it should come after the threshing shed, the cow barn, the stable.

Jefferson believed that the great advances of science since the Enlightenment should better man's condition in other realms as well as the physical, especially here in America, where we had sloughed off the inertia and tradition that for so long had obstructed Europeans. Did it work out that way? Well, a few years ago when Calvin Coolidge asseverated that the business of America is business, few laughed. Even fewer wept.

Jefferson *believed*. That might be all that is needed. He believed in his fellowmen, whom Hamilton despised. It is impossible to love somebody who despises you, but Americans at least have given Alexander Hamilton a monumental share of their admiration.

The whole thing, it might be said, constitutes a Mexican standoff, a tie. Neither man won, at least not at the cost of the other. Yet each won what he would have valued most. Hamilton we keep on our ten-dollar bills, but Jefferson we keep in our hearts.

★ Bibliography ★

Adams, Henry, *History of the United States of America During the Administration of Thomas Jefferson.* 2 volumes. New York: Albert and Charles Boni, 1930.

—— *John Randolph.* Boston: Houghton Mifflin Co., 1910.

—— *The Life of Albert Gallatin.* New York: Peter Smith, 1943.

Adams, John, *The Works of John Adams, with Life,* edited by Charles Francis Adams. 10 volumes. Boston: Little, Brown & Co., 1850–56.

Agar, Herbert, *The People's Choice, from Washington to Harding: A Study in Democracy.* Boston: Houghton Mifflin Company, 1933.

—— *The Price of Union.* Boston: Houghton Mifflin Co., 1950.

Alberts, Robert C., "The Notorious Affair of Mrs. Reynolds." *American Heritage,* February 1973.

Alexander, DeAlva Stanwood, *A Political History of the State of New York.* 3 volumes. New York: Henry Holt and Company, 1906.

Alexander, Edward P., *A Revolutionary Conservative: James Duane of New York.* New York: Columbia University Press, 1938.

Allen, Gardner W., *Our Naval War with France.* Boston: Houghton Mifflin Company, 1909.

Allison, John Murray, *Adams and Jefferson: The Story of a Friendship.* Norman, Okla.: University of Oklahoma Press, 1966.

Anderson, Frank M., "Contemporary Opinion of the Virginia and Kentucky Resolutions." *American Historical Review,* Vol. 5, Nos. 1 and 2, 1899 and 1900.

—— "The Enforcement of the Alien and Sedition Laws." *Annual Report of the American Historical Association 1912.* Washington: The Smithsonian Institution, 1914.

Atherton, Gertrude, "The Hunt for Hamilton's Mother." *North American Review,* Vol. 175, 1902.

Baldwin, Leland, *Whiskey Rebels: The Story of a Frontier Uprising.* Pittsburgh: University of Pittsburgh Press, 1939.

Bancroft, George, *History of the Formation of the Constitution of the United States.* 2 volumes. New York: D. Appleton and Company, 1882.

Bassett, John Spencer, *The Federalist System, 1789–1801.* New York and London: Harper and Brothers Publishers, 1906.

Beard, Charles A., *Economic Interpretation of the Constitution.* New York: The Macmillan Company, 1957.

——— *Economic Origins of Jeffersonian Democracy.* New York: The Macmillan Company, 1927.

Becker, Carl, "What Is Still Living in the Political Philosophy of Thomas Jefferson." *American Historical Review,* Vol. XLVIII, No. 4, July 1943.

Beloff, Max, *Thomas Jefferson and American Democracy.* London: Hodder & Stoughton Limited, 1948.

Bemis, Samuel Flagg, *Jay's Treaty: A Study in Commerce and Diplomacy.* New York: The Macmillan Company, 1923.

——— *Pinckney's Treaty: A Study of America's Advantage from Europe's Distress, 1783–1800.* Baltimore: Johns Hopkins University Press, 1926.

——— "The Background of Washington's Foreign Policy." *Yale Review,* New Series, Vol. XVI, 1927.

Bernhard, Winfred E. A., *Fisher Ames, Federalist and Statesman, 1758–1808.* Chapel Hill, N.C.: University of North Carolina Press, 1965.

Bethea, Andrew J., *The Contribution of Charles Pinckney to the Formation of the American Union.* Richmond, Va.: Garret & Massie, Inc., 1937.

Beveridge, Albert J., *The Life of John Marshall.* 4 volumes. Boston and New York: Houghton Mifflin Company, 1929.

Binkley, Wilfred E., *American Political Parties: Their Natural History.* New York: Alfred A. Knopf, 1947.

Binney, Horace, *An Inquiry into the Formation of Washington's Farewell Address.* New York: DaCapo Press, 1969.

Bond, Beverly W., Jr. *The Monroe Mission to France, 1794–1796.* Baltimore: The Johns Hopkins Press, 1907.

Borden, Morton, *Parties and Politics in the Early Republic, 1789–1815.* New York: Thomas Y. Crowell Company, 1967.

Bourne, Edward G., "Authorship of the Federalist," *American Historical Review,* Vol. II, Nos. 3 and 4.

Bowers, Claude G., *Jefferson and Hamilton: The Struggle for Democracy in America.* Boston: Houghton Mifflin Company, 1926.

——— *Jefferson in Power: The Death Struggle of Federalists.* Boston: Houghton Mifflin Company, 1936.

Boyd, Julian P., *Number 7: Alexander Hamilton's Secret Attempts to Control American Foreign Policy.* Princeton, N.J.: Princeton University Press, 1964.

Brant, Irving, "Edmund Randolph, Not Guilty!" *William and Mary Quarterly,* 3rd series, Vol. VII, No. 2 (April 1950).

——— *James Madison: Father of the Constitution, 1787–1800.* Indianapolis, Ind.: The Bobbs-Merrill Company, 1950.

——— *Storm over the Constitution.* Indianapolis, Ind.: The Bobbs-Merrill Company, 1936.

Brodie, Fawn M., "The Great Jefferson Taboo." *American Heritage,* June 1972.

Brown, Robert E., *Charles Beard and the Constitution: A Critical Analysis of "An Economic Interpretation of the Constitution."* Princeton, N.J.: Princeton University Press, 1956.

Bryce, James, *The American Commonwealth.* 2 volumes. Chicago: Charles H. Sergel & Co., 1891.

——— "The Predictions of Hamilton and De Tocqueville." *Johns Hopkins University Studies in Historical and Political Science.* 5th Series, Vol. IX (September 1887).

Burnett, Edmund C., ed., *Letters of Members of the Continental Congress.* 8 volumes. Washington, D.C.: Carnegie Institute of Washington, 1921–36.

Burt, A. I., *The United States, Great Britain and British North America from the Revolution to the Establishment of Peace After the War of 1812.* New Haven: Yale University Press, 1940.

Chambers, William Nisbet, *Political Parties in a New Nation: The American Experience, 1776–1809.* New York: Oxford University Press, 1963.

——— and Burnham, Walter Dean, eds., *The American Party Systems: Stages of Political Development.* New York: Oxford University Press, 1967.

Channing, Edward, *The Jeffersonian System, 1801–1811.* New York and London: Harper & Brothers Publishers, 1906.

Charles, Joseph, *The Origins of the American Party System*. Williamsburg, Va.: Institute of Early American History and Culture, 1956.

Chinard, Gilbert, *Honest John Adams*. Boston: Little, Brown and Company, 1933.

Coleman, William, *A Collection of the Facts and Documents Relative to the Death of Major-General Alexander Hamilton*. New York: I. Riley and Co., 1804.

Commager, Henry Steele, ed., *Documents of American History*. (5th edition) New York: Appleton-Century-Crofts, Inc., 1948.

Cooke, Jacob E., ed., *The Federalist: America's Greatest Contribution to Political Philosophy*. Middletown, Conn.: Wesleyan University Press, 1961.

Corwin, Edward S., *French Policy and the American Alliance of 1778*. Princeton, N.J.: Princeton University Press, 1916.

Coupland, Richard, *The Quebec Act: A Study in Statesmanship*. Oxford: Oxford University Press, 1925.

Craven, Wesley Frank, *The Legend of the Founding Fathers*. New York: New York University Press, 1956.

Cunliffe, Marcus, *The Nation Takes Shape, 1789–1837*. Chicago: University of Chicago Press, 1959.

Cunningham, Noble E., *The Jeffersonian Republicans: The Formation of Party Organization, 1789–1801*. Chapel Hill, N.C.: University of North Carolina Press, 1957.

Darling, Arthur Burr, *Our Rising Empire, 1763–1803*. New Haven: Yale University Press, 1940.

Dauer, Manning J., *The Adams Federalists*. Baltimore: The Johns Hopkins Press, 1953.

Davis, Rich Dewey, *Financial History of the United States*. New York: Longmans, Green and Co., 1925.

DeConde, Alexander, *Entangling Alliance: Politics & Diplomacy Under George Washington*. Durham, N.C.: Duke University Press, 1958.

———— *The Quasi-War: The Politics and Diplomacy of the Undeclared War with France, 1797–1801*. New York: Charles Scribner's Sons, 1966.

———— "Washington's Farewell, the French Alliance, and the Election of 1796," *Mississippi Valley Historical Review*, Vol. XXXIV, No. 3 (December 1947).

Drake, Francis Samuel, *Life and Correspondence of Henry Knox*. Boston: S. G. Drake, 1873.

Dunbar, Louise Burnham, *A Study of "Monarchical" Tendencies in the United States from 1776 to 1801*. Urbana, Ill.: University of Illinois Studies in the Social Sciences, Vol. X, No. 1 (March 1922).

Duniway, Clyde Augustus, "French Influence on the Adoption of the Federal Constitution," *American Historical Review,* Vol. IX, No. 1.

Farrand, Max, *Framing the Constitution of the United States.* New Haven, Conn.: Yale University Press, 1930.

———— *The Fathers of the Constitution: A Chronicle of the Establishment of the Union.* New Haven, Conn.: Yale University Press, 1921.

———— editor. *The Records of the Federal Convention of 1787.* 3 volumes. New Haven, Conn.: Yale University Press, 1911.

Faulkner, Harold Underwood, *American Economic History.* New York: Harper & Brothers, 1931.

Faÿ, Bernard, "Early Party Machinery in the United States: Pennsylvania in the Election of 1796," *The Pennsylvania Magazine of History and Biography.* Volume LX, No. 4 (October 1936).

———— *The Revolutionary Spirit in France and America: A Study of Moral and Intellectual Relations Between France and the United States at the End of the Eighteenth Century.* New York: Harcourt, Brace and Company, 1927.

———— *The Two Franklins: Fathers of American Democracy.* Boston: Little, Brown and Company, 1933.

Fish, Carl Russell, *The Civil Service and the Patronage.* Cambridge, Mass: Harvard University Press, 1920.

Fiske, John, *The Critical Period of American History.* Boston and New York: Houghton, Mifflin and Company, 1898.

Fletcher, Mildred Stahl, "Louisiana as a Factor in French Diplomacy from 1763 to 1800," *Mississippi Valley Historical Review,* Vol. XVII.

Flexner, James Thomas, *George Washington: Anguish and Farewell, 1793–1799.* Boston: Little, Brown and Company, 1969.

Ford, Henry Jones, *Alexander Hamilton.* New York: Charles Scribner's Sons, 1931.

———— *Washington and His Colleagues: A Chronicle of the Rise and Fall of Federalism.* New Haven, Conn.: Yale University Press, 1920.

Ford, Paul Leicester, "The Authorship of the Federalist," *American Historical Review*, Vol. II, No. 4.

Freeman, Douglas Southall, with John Alexander Carroll and Mary Wells Ashworth, *George Washington: A Biography*, Vol. VII, *First in Peace*. New York: Charles Scribner's Sons, 1957.

Gibbs, George, *Memoirs of the Administrations of Washington and John Adams*. New York: Printed for the subscribers, 1846.

Gould, F. J., *Thomas Paine, 1737–1809*. Boston: Small, Maynard and Co., 1925.

Govan, Thomas P., "The Rich, the Well-Born, and Alexander Hamilton," *Mississippi Valley Historical Review*, Vol. XXXVI, No. 4 (March 1950).

Greene, Evarts B., and Harrington, Virginia D., *American Population Before the Federal Census of 1790*. New York: Columbia University Press, 1932.

Griswold, Rufus Wilmot, *The Republican Court; or, American Society in the Days of Washington*. New York: Haskell House Publishers Ltd., 1971.

Hamilton, Alexander, "Alexander Hamilton's Notes on the Convention of 1787," Worthington Chauncey Ford, ed., *American Historical Review*, Vol. X.

——— *Letter from Alexander Hamilton Concerning the Public Conduct and Character of John Adams, Esq., President of the United States*. Boston: E. G. House, 1809.

———*The Works of Alexander Hamilton*, John C. Hamilton, ed. 7 volumes. New York: J. F. Trow, 1850–51.

——— *The Works of Alexander Hamilton*, Henry Cabot Lodge, ed. 12 volumes. New York: G. P. Putnam's Sons, 1904.

Hamilton, Allan McLane, *The Intimate Life of Alexander Hamilton*. New York: Charles Scribner's Sons, 1910.

Hamilton, John C., *Life of Alexander Hamilton*. 7 volumes. Boston: Houghton, Osgood and Company, 1879.

Hammond, Bray, *Banks and Politics in America from the Revolution to the Civil War*. Princeton, N.J.: Princeton University Press, 1957.

Handler, Edward, *America and Europe in the Political Thought of John Adams*. Cambridge, Mass.: Harvard University Press, 1964.

Hazen, Charles Downer, *Contemporary American Opinion of the French Revolution*. Baltimore: The Johns Hopkins Press, 1897.

Heinlein, Jay C., "Albert Gallatin: A Pioneer in Public Administration," *William and Mary Quarterly,* 3rd Series, Vol. VII, No. 1.

Hemphill, W. Edwin, "The Jeffersonian Background of the Louisiana Purchase," *Mississippi Valley Historical Review,* Vol. XXII, No. 1.

Hofstadter, Richard, "Beard and the Constitution: The History of an Idea." *American Quarterly.* Fall 1950.

―――― *The American Political Tradition.* New York: Alfred A. Knopf, 1954.

Howe, John R., Jr., *The Changing Political Thought of John Adams.* Princeton, N.J.: Princeton University Press, 1966.

Hutchinson, J. R., *The Press-Gang, Afloat and Ashore.* New York: E. P. Dutton & Co., 1914.

Jacobs, James Ripley, *The Beginning of the U.S. Army, 1783–1812.* Port Washington, N.Y.: Kennikat Press, 1972.

Jefferson, Thomas, *The Papers of Thomas Jefferson,* Julian P. Boyd, ed. 13 volumes. Princeton, N.J.: Princeton University Press, 1950.

Jensen, Merrill, *The Articles of Confederation: An Interpretation of the Social-Constitutional History of the American Revolution, 1774–1781.* Madison, Wis.: University of Wisconsin Press, 1940.

―――― *The New Nation: A History of the United States During the Confederation, 1781–1789.* New York: Alfred A. Knopf, 1950.

Kaplan, Lawrence S., *Jefferson and France: An Essay on Politics and Political Ideas.* New Haven, Conn.: Yale University Press, 1967.

Kaufman, Burton Ira, ed., *Washington's Farewell Address: The View from the 20th Century.* Chicago: Quadrangle Books, 1969.

Key, Vladimir Orlando, *Politics, Parties, and Pressure Groups.* New York: Thomas Y. Crowell Company, 1961.

Kilroe, Edwin P., *Saint Tammany and the Origin of the Society of Tammany or Columbian Order in the City of New York.* New York: Columbia University Press, 1913.

Koch, Adrienne, *Jefferson and Madison: The Great Collaboration.* New York: Alfred A. Knopf, Inc., 1950.

Kurtz, Stephen G., *The Presidency of John Adams: The Collapse of Federalism, 1795–1800.* Philadelphia: University of Pennsylvania Press, 1957.

Kyte, George W., "A Spy on the Western Waters: The Military Intelligence Mission of General Collot in 1796," *Mississippi Valley Historical Review,* Vol. XXXIV, No. 3 (December 1947).

Leary, Lewis, *That Rascal Freneau: A Study in Literary Failure.* New Brunswick, N.J.: Rutgers University Press, 1941.

Levy, Leonard W., *Jefferson and Civil Liberties: The Darker Side.* Cambridge, Mass.: Harvard University Press, 1963.

Libby, Orin Grant, *The Geographical Distribution of the Vote of the Thirteen States on the Federal Constitution, 1787–88.* Madison, Wis.: University of Wisconsin Press, 1894.

Link, Eugene Perry, *Democratic-Republican Societies, 1790–1800.* New York: Columbia University Press, 1942.

Lodge, Henry Cabot, *Alexander Hamilton.* Boston: Houghton, Mifflin and Company, 1898.

———— ed., *The Works of Alexander Hamilton.* 9 volumes. New York: G. P. Putnam's Sons, 1885–86.

Looze, Helene Johnson, *Alexander Hamilton and the British Orientation of American Foreign Policy, 1783–1803.* The Hague, Netherlands: Mouton & Co., 1969.

Luetscher, George D., *Early Political Machinery in the United States.* Philadelphia: University of Pennsylvania Press, 1903.

Lynch, William O., *Fifty Years of Party Warfare, 1789–1837.* Indianapolis, Ind.: The Bobbs-Merrill Company, 1931.

Lyon, E. Wilson, "The Directory and the United States," *American Historical Review,* Vol. XLIII, No. 3 (April 1938).

Lyon, Hastings, *The Constitution and the Men Who Made It: The Story of the Constitutional Convention, 1787.* Boston: Houghton Mifflin Company, 1936.

McCaleb, Walter Flavius, *The Aaron Burr Conspiracy* and *A New Light on Aaron Burr.* New York: Argosy-Antiquarian, Ltd., 1966.

McDonald, Forrest, *We the People: The Economic Origins of the Constitution.* Chicago: University of Chicago Press, 1958.

McLaughlin, Andrew Cunningham, *The Confederation and the Constitution, 1783–1789.* New York: Harper and Brothers, 1905.

McLemore, R. A., "Jeffersonian Diplomacy in the Purchase of Louisiana, 1803." *Louisiana Historical Quarterly,* Vol. 18 (1935).

Madison, James, *Journal of the Federal Convention,* E. H. Scott, ed. 2 volumes. Chicago: Albert, Scott and Company, 1894.

———— *The Debates in the Federal Convention of 1787 Which Framed the Constitution of the United States of America,* Gaillard Hunt and James Brown Scott, eds. New York: Oxford University Press, 1920.

———— *The Writings of James Madison,* Gaillard Hunt, ed. 9 volumes. New York: G. P. Putnam's Sons, 1901.

Mahan, Alfred Thayer, *The Influence of Sea Power upon the French Revolution and Empire, 1793–1812.* 2 volumes. Boston: Little, Brown and Company, 1919.

Main, Jackson Turner, *The Antifederalists: Critics of the Constitution, 1781–1788.* Chapel Hill, N.C.: University of North Carolina Press, 1961.

Malone, Dumas, *Jefferson and the Ordeal of Liberty.* Boston: Little, Brown and Company, 1962.

———— *Jefferson and the Rights of Man.* Boston: Little, Brown and Company, 1951.

Marsh, Philip, "Hamilton and Monroe," *Mississippi Valley Historical Review,* Vol. XXXIV, No. 3 (December 1947).

———— "John Beckley—Mystery Man of the Early Jeffersonians," *The Pennsylvania Magazine of History and Biography,* Vol. LXXII, No. 1 (January 1948).

———— *Philip Freneau, Poet and Journalist.* Minneapolis, Minn.: Dillon Press, 1967.

———— "Philip Freneau and His Circle," *The Pennsylvania Magazine of History and Biography,* Vol. LXIII, No. 1 (January 1939).

———— "Randolph and Hamilton," *The Pennsylvania Magazine of History and Biography.* Vol. LXXII, No. 3 (July 1948).

Miller, Hunter, ed., *Treaties and Other International Acts of the United States of America.* 8 volumes. Washington, D.C.: Government Printing Office, 1931.

Miller, John C., *Alexander Hamilton: Portrait in Paradox.* New York: Harper & Brothers, Publishers, 1959.

———— *Crisis in Freedom: The Alien and Sedition Acts.* Boston: Little, Brown and Company, 1951.

———— *The Federalist Era, 1789–1801.* New York: Harper & Brothers, 1960.

Miller, William, "First Fruits of Republican Organization: Political Aspects of the Congressional Election of 1794," *William and Mary Quarterly,* Vol. LXIII, No. 2 (April 1939).

———— "The Democratic Societies and the Whiskey Rebellion," *The Pennsylvania Magazine of History and Biography,* Vol. LXII, No. 3 (July 1938).

Miner, C. E., *The Ratification of the Federal Constitution by the State of New York*. New York: Columbia University Press, 1921.

Minnigerode, Meade, *Jefferson, Friend of France, 1793; The Career of Edmund Charles Genêt, 1763–1834*. New York and London: G. P. Putnam's Sons, 1928.

Mitchell, Broadus, *Alexander Hamilton: The National Adventure. 1788–1804*. New York: The Macmillan Company, 1962.

———— *Heritage from Hamilton*. New York: Columbia University Press, 1957.

Monaghan, Frank, *John Jay*. Indianapolis, Ind.: The Bobbs-Merrill Company, Inc., 1935.

Morison, Samuel Eliot, *Harrison Gray Otis, Federalist, 1765–1848*. 2 volumes. Boston: Houghton Mifflin Company, 1913.

Morris, Richard B., *The Peacemakers: The Great Powers and American Independence*. New York: Harper & Row, 1965.

Morse, John T., Jr., *James Monroe, 1776 to 1826*. Boston: Houghton Mifflin and Company, 1883.

———— *John Adams*. Boston: Houghton Mifflin and Company, 1899.

Mudge, Eugene Tenbroeck, *The Social Philosophy of John Taylor of Caroline: A Study in Jeffersonian Democracy*. New York: Columbia University Press, 1939.

Myers, Gustavus, *The History of Tammany Hall*. New York: Boni and Liveright, 1917.

Nichols, Roy F., *The Invention of the American Political Parties: A Study of Political Improvisation*. New York: The Macmillan Company, 1967.

Oberholtzer, Ellis Paxson, *Robert Morris: Patriot and Financier*. New York: The Macmillan Company, 1903.

Oliver, Frederick Scott, *Alexander Hamilton: An Essay on American Union*. New York: G. P. Putnam's Sons, 1907.

Palmer, Robert Roswell, *The Age of the Democratic Revolution: A Political History of Europe and America, 1760–1800*. 2 volumes. Princeton, N.J.: Princeton University Press, 1964.

Paltsits, Victor Hugo, *Washington's Farewell Address*. New York: The New York Public Library, 1935.

Pancake, John S., "Aaron Burr: Would-Be Usurper," *William and Mary Quarterly*. 3rd Series, Vol. VIII, No. 2.

Parton, James, *The Life and Times of Aaron Burr*. 5th edition. New York: Mason Brothers, 1858.

Pellew, George, *John Jay*. Boston: Houghton Mifflin & Co., 1890.

Perkins, Bradford, *The First Rapprochement: England and the United States, 1795–1805*. Berkeley and Los Angeles: University of California Press, 1955.

Peterson, Merrill D., *The Jefferson Image in the American Mind*. New York: Oxford University Press, 1960.

———— *Thomas Jefferson and the New Nation: A Biography*. New York: Oxford University Press, 1970.

Powell, J. H., *Bring Out Your Dead: The Great Plague of Yellow Fever in Philadelphia in 1793*. Philadelphia: University of Pennsylvania Press, 1949.

Riethmuller, Christopher James, *Alexander Hamilton and His Contemporaries; or, The Rise of the American Constitution*. London: Bell and Daldy, 1864.

Rippy, J. Fred, and Debo, Angie, *The Historical Background of the American Policy of Isolation*. Northampton, Mass.: Smith College Studies in History, April–July 1924.

Risjord, Norman K., *The Early American Party System*. New York: Harper & Row, 1969.

Roosevelt, Theodore, *Gouverneur Morris*. Boston: Houghton Mifflin and Company, 1891.

Rossiter, Clinton, *Seedtime of the Republic: The Origin of the American Tradition of Political Liberty*. New York: Harcourt, Brace & Co., 1953.

Rutland, Robert Allen, *The Birth of the Bill of Rights, 1776–1791*. Chapel Hill, N. C.: University of North Carolina Press, 1955.

St. Mery, Moreau De, *Moreau de St. Mery's American Journey, 1793–1798*, Kenneth Roberts and Anna M. Roberts, trans. and eds. Garden City, N.Y.: Doubleday & Company, Inc., 1947.

Schachner, Nathan, *Aaron Burr: A Biography*. New York: Frederick A. Stokes Company, 1937.

———— *Alexander Hamilton*. New York and London: D. Appleton-Century Company, Inc., 1946.

Schmucker, Samuel M., *The Life and Times of Alexander Hamilton*. Philadelphia: J. W. Bradley, 1859.

Seabury, Rev. Samuel, *Letters of a Westchester Farmer (1774–1775)*, Clarence H. Vance, ed. White Plains, N.Y.: Westchester County Historical Society, 1930.

Smith, James Morton, *Freedom's Fetters: The Alien and Sedition Laws and American Civil Liberties*. Ithaca, N.Y.: Cornell University Press, 1956.

Spaulding, E. Wilder, *New York in the Critical Period, 1783–1789*. New York: Columbia University Press, 1954.

Stille, Charles J., *The Life and Times of John Dickinson, 1732–1808*. Philadelphia: Historical Society of Pennsylvania, 1891.

Sumner, Charles Graham, *The Financier and the Finances of the American Revolution*. 2 volumes. New York: Dodd, Mead and Company, 1891.

Sumner, William Graham, *Alexander Hamilton*. New York: Dodd, Mead and Company, 1890.

Swiggett, Howard, *The Extraordinary Mr. Morris*. Garden City, N.Y.: Doubleday and Co., 1952.

Syrett, Harold C., ed., *The Papers of Alexander Hamilton*. 15 volumes. New York: Columbia University Press, 1961–69.

———— and Cooke, Jean G., eds., *Interview in Weehawken: The Burr-Hamilton Duel, as Told in the Original Documents*. With an introduction and conclusion by Willard M. Wallace. Middletown, Conn.: Wesleyan University Press, 1960.

Tansill, Charles Callan, ed., *Documents Illustrative of the Formation of the Union of the American States*. Washington, D.C.: Government Printing Office, 1927.

Thomas, Charles Marion, *American Neutrality in 1793: A Study in Cabinet Government*. New York: Columbia University Press, 1931.

Tolles, Frederick B., "Unofficial Ambassador: George Logan's Mission to France, 1798," *William and Mary Quarterly*, 3rd Series, Vol. VII, No. 1 (January 1950).

Tugwell, Rexford Guy, and Dorfman, Joseph, "Alexander Hamilton: Nation-Maker," *Columbia University Quarterly*, Vol. XXIX (1937) and Vol. XXX (1938).

Turner, Frederick Jackson, "The Origin of Genêt's Projected Attack on Louisiana and the Floridas," *American Historical Review*, Vol. III.

Van Alstyne, Richard W., "The Significance of the Mississippi Valley in American Diplomatic History, 1686–1890," *Mississippi Valley Historical Review*, Vol. XXXVI, No. 2 (September 1949).

Van Der Linden, Frank, *The Turning Point: Jefferson's Battle for the Presidency*. Washington, D.C.: Robert B. Luce, Inc., 1962.

Ver Steeg, Clarence L., *Robert Morris: Revolutionary Financier*. Philadelphia: University of Pennsylvania Press, 1954.

Walsh, Correa Moylan, *The Political Science of John Adams: A Study in the Theory of Mixed Government and the Bicameral System*. New York: G. P. Putnam's Sons, 1915.

Wandell, Samuel H., and Minnigerode, Meade, *Aaron Burr*. New York and London: G. P. Putnam's Sons, 1927.

Warren, Charles, *Jacobin and Junto, or, Early American Politics as Viewed in the Diary of Dr. Nathaniel Ames, 1758–1822*. Cambridge, Mass.: Harvard University Press, 1931.

Washington, George, *The Writings of George Washington, from the Original Manuscript Sources, 1745–1799*, John C. Fitzpatrick, ed. 39 volumes. Washington, D.C.: U.S. Government Printing Office, 1931–44.

Weyl, Nathaniel, *Treason: The Story of Disloyalty and Betrayal in American History*. Washington, D.C.: Public Affairs Press, 1950.

Woodbury, Margaret, *Public Opinion in Philadelphia, 1789–1801*. Northampton, Mass.: Smith College Studies in History, October 1919–January 1920.

Woolery, William K., "The Relation of Thomas Jefferson to American Foreign Policy, 1783–1795," Johns Hopkins Studies in Historical and Political Science, Vol. XLV (1927).

Index

Date Due